Phonics Activities for Early Literacy

A Sound Way

Elizabeth Love & Sue Reilly

Pembroke Publishers Limited

Pembroke Publishers Limited
538 Hood Road,
Markham, Ontario, Canada L3R 3K9

© Addison Wesley Longman Australia 1996
This edition of A Sound Way (First Edition) is published by
arrangement with Addison Wesley Longman Australia Pty. Ltd.,
Melbourne, Australia.

Designed by Kikitsa Michalantos
Illustrated by Jean Cooper-Brown

Thanks to Linda Hart-Hewins for her assistance with this special
Canadian edition.

Canadian Cataloguing in Publication Data

Love, Elizabeth, 1950-
 A sound way : phonics activities for early literacy

1st Canadian ed.
Includes bibliographical references and index.
ISBN 1-55138-079-X

1. Reading – Phonetic method.   2. English language –
Phonetics – Problems, exercises, etc.   I. Reilly, Sue,
1950- . II. Title.

LB1573.3.L68 1996   372.4'145   C96-931290-3

Printed and bound in Canada on acid-free paper.
10 9 8 7 6 5 4 3 2

Foreword

Communication is the main goal of oral language.
Young children develop their language skills by
hearing the spoken language of their parents.
Children are encouraged to understand what is
said, follow directions, answer questions, tell
what happened, comment or ask questions.
Establishing meaning is the major focus of this
interaction.

For readers and writers the aim of written
communication is also the establishment of
meaning. The transition from competence as a
speaker and listener to competence as a reader
and writer can sometimes be a slow and difficult
process — it requires the acquisition of a new
language skill.

During the process of learning to read, spell
and write, the child must begin to think about the
structure and components of spoken language.
This is called **metalinguistic awareness**. It
involves knowing that a sentence is made up of
words, which in turn are made up of a sequence
of sounds. It also includes talking about what
words mean and recognizing correct grammar.

An important aspect of metalinguistic awareness
is the ability to manipulate sounds within words.
This is called **phonological awareness**.

Phonological awareness builds upon the child's
primary language and cognitive growth and is
facilitated by language experience at home and
school and through reading. Research has shown
that phonological awareness is the most powerful
predictor of success in learning to read and spell
(Share, Jorm, Maclean and Matthews, 1984).
Training in this awareness has been shown to
positively influence the development of beginning
reading and writing skills (Wagner and Torgeson,
1987).

However, phonological awareness is only one
of many strategies to teach children to read and
write. This book's aim is to provide key language
and phonological awareness activities that can be
used together with existing lessons plans, as part
of the classroom language program

Contents

· ·

About the Book

A Sound Way is divided into four sections.

The first two sections are **What's In A Sound?** and **Sound–Letter Link**. Studies have shown that phonological awareness can be taught, and that this teaching is more effective when sound-awareness activities are linked at an early stage with sound-letter training (Bradley and Bryant, 1985). It is for this reason that we have included these two important sections for the teacher prior to the section on **Phonological Awareness**.

This book concludes with a **Teacher Resource** section.

What's In A Sound?

This section provides information and activities about sounds: where and how they are made and which ones are easily confused. It includes practical activities to help children learn about sounds in a fun way. Be sure not to overlook **What's In A Sound?** as knowledge in this area is basic to all phonological awareness activities.

Sound-Letter Link

In this section teachers are shown ways of assisting children to acquire clear concepts of sounds and letters, thus enabling children to make firm associations between the two. Similarly the **Sound-Letter Link** section is crucial if children are to succeed with reading and spelling tasks.

Note: It is important for the children's helper to be very familiar with all the sections of the book so that planning of developmentally appropriate, rather than random, activities can occur.

Phonological Awareness

There are seven main areas involved in building phonological awareness.

1 Word Awareness (including compound words) This involves breaking sentences up into words. Compound words are divided into their meaningful parts.

2 Syllables
Words can be broken into syllables or beats.

3 Rhyme
This requires recognition and production of words that rhyme. That is, words that end with the same group of sounds.

4 Alliteration
Alliteration involves providing words that begin with the same sound as a given target word. It assumes a beginning-sound analysis skill.

5 Analysis
This refers to the isolation of sounds within words — in the initial, medial and final positions. It also includes discovering how many sounds are in words, and working out the component sounds of consonant blends.

6 Blending
In this section, individual parts of words, either the syllables or sounds, are given and the child is required to 'push them together' and discover the whole word.

7 Manipulation
These tasks require the sounds in words to be moved from one position to another.

Note: These seven sections are in a general developmental order of difficulty; however, this does not preclude working on more than one section at a time. For example: the oral activities in **Blending** are best presented prior to, or in conjunction with, those for **Sound Analysis**.

Oral and Written/Reading Activities

Within each of the above areas of phonological awareness there are two levels of activities: oral and written.

Oral

Beginning activities involve recognition and matching. For example: 'Do these words start with the same sound?' 'Which of these three words does not rhyme?'

Later activities require independent production of a word, sound or sentence. For example: 'Tell me a word that ends with the sound 's'.' As these activities involve only talking and listening (and not reading or writing) they are symbolized by an open mouth.

Written/Reading

These activities assume sound-awareness skill at the oral level and some letter-sound knowledge. They involve some reading and writing and are symbolized by a pencil.

Note: Many written/reading activities can be made easier by presenting the material orally or with picture support.

About the Activities

• •

- The purchaser of this book may photocopy the activity sheets for individual, small group or classroom use.

- The activities can be used as individual worksheets for children. Activities can also be used by teachers to evaluate individual and class progress.

- Use activities as whole-class assignments sparingly because students' levels are varied.

- The **Extensions** (featured at the bottom of selected activities) offer opportunities for children to use creative-thinking and problem-solving skills. These activities are well-suited for partner and small group work.

- The picture card sheets can be backed with heavy card and laminated to produce a permanent class resource.

- Care should be taken to match appropriate activities to the child's ability. Parents should be guided by their child's teacher or speech pathologist in the selection of appropriate activities.

- Teacher resource pages are found throughout the book.
  Additional information about suitable books, tapes and games can be found in the **Resource List** at the end of this book.

- The **Phonological Awareness Activities Checklist** that follows presents a developmental continuum of sound awareness. Teachers can use the checklist as a tracking sheet to help assess individual student success.

Phonological Awareness Activities Checklist

• •

(* = photocopiable worksheet/activity)   Student's Name _____

Activity	Oral/ Written	Page	Evaluation	
			Completed	Comments
Word Awareness				
Breaking Up A Sentence	👄	48	_____	_____
Breaking Sentences	👄	49	_____	_____
Rearranging Sentences	👄	50	_____	_____
*What's Left 1	👄	51	_____	_____
*What's Left 2	👄	52	_____	_____
*Make Your Own Words	👄	54	_____	_____
*Make Your Own Words Again	👄	55	_____	_____
*Sentence Cut Ups	✏	56	_____	_____
*Build Up Sentences	✏	57	_____	_____
*'Go Togethers'	✏	58	_____	_____
*Divide	✏	59	_____	_____
*Compound Words	✏	60	_____	_____
*Word Match-Up	✏	61	_____	_____
*Compound Corner	✏	63	_____	_____
*Compound Racetrack	✏	64	_____	_____
*Two in One	✏	65	_____	_____
Syllables				
*Syllable Signs	👄	68	_____	_____
*Say and Colour	👄	69	_____	_____
Clap and Move to Syllables	👄	70	_____	_____
*What's in a Name?	👄	72	_____	_____
*Syllable Search	✏	73	_____	_____
*Syllables	✏	74	_____	_____
*Long Words Made Simple	✏	75	_____	_____
*Counting on Frank	✏	76	_____	_____
*Prefix Power	✏	77	_____	_____
*Mixed-Up Syllables	✏	78	_____	_____
*Target Practice	✏	79	_____	_____
*Syllable Clues	✏	80	_____	_____
*The Longest Word	✏	81	_____	_____
Rhyming				
Rhyming — Same or Different?	👄	84	_____	_____
Three Word Rhyme	👄	85	_____	_____
*Colour Rhyme 1	👄	87	_____	_____
*Rhyming Snap	👄	88	_____	_____
*Draw a Rhyme 1	👄	91	_____	_____
Follow That Rhyme	👄	93	_____	_____
*Rhyming Pairs 1	👄	94	_____	_____
*Rhyming Pairs 2	👄	95	_____	_____
A Rhyme in Time	👄	96	_____	_____
*The Rhymers	👄	97	_____	_____
*My Rhyming Pictures	👄	99	_____	_____
*Odd Man Out	👄	100	_____	_____
*My Rhyming Words	👄	102	_____	_____

4

Phonological Awareness Activities Checklist

· ·

(* = photocopiable worksheet/activity)   Student's Name _____

Activity	Oral/ Written	Page	Evaluation	
			Completed	Comments
*Draw a Rhyme 2	╱	103	_____	_____
*Colour Rhyme 2	╱	104	_____	_____
*Climb & Rhyme	╱	105	_____	_____
*Rhyming Bubbles	╱	106	_____	_____
*Re-Rhyme Humpty Dumpty	╱	107	_____	_____
*Rhyming Sentences	╱	108	_____	_____
*Look-Alikes — Do They Rhyme?	╱	109	_____	_____
*Rhyming Challenge	╱	110	_____	_____
Alliteration				
Sound Stories 1	⬒	112	_____	_____
Sneaky Sounds	⬒	112	_____	_____
'I Went Shopping and I Bought'	⬒	113	_____	_____
*Sound Stories 2	╱	114	_____	_____
*Football Favourites	╱	115	_____	_____
*Jobs	╱	116	_____	_____
*Bad Habits	╱	117	_____	_____
*Good Habits	╱	118	_____	_____
*Alliterative Sentences	╱	119	_____	_____
Analysis				
Listening Corner	⬒	122	_____	_____
Sound Bucket Game	⬒	123	_____	_____
Copy Cat	⬒	124	_____	_____
*Hear Well?	⬒	125	_____	_____
*First Sound Snap 1	⬒	126	_____	_____
*First Sound Dominoes	⬒	130	_____	_____
*Odd First Sound Out	⬒	134	_____	_____
Thinking With Language	⬒	138	_____	_____
Tails	⬒	139	_____	_____
*What's In the Last Carriage?	⬒	140	_____	_____
Sorting Sounds and Letters	⬒	141	_____	_____
Keep It Concrete	⬒	142	_____	_____
Keep It Concrete	╱	143	_____	_____
Feel and Find the Sounds	⬒	144	_____	_____
*Little Bits of Words 1	⬒	145	_____	_____
*Little Bits of Words 2	⬒	146	_____	_____
*How Many Sounds?	⬒	147	_____	_____
*Grids	⬒	148	_____	_____
*Cut and Sort	⬒	151	_____	_____
*Long or Short	⬒	152	_____	_____
Find the Short Vowels	⬒	153	_____	_____
Find the Long Vowels	⬒	154	_____	_____
Long or Short Vowels?	⬒	155	_____	_____
Short Vowel Search	⬒	157	_____	_____
*Rolly the Rabbit	⬒	158	_____	_____

Phonological Awareness Activities Checklist

(* = photocopiable worksheet/activity)   Student's Name _____

Activity	Oral/ Written	Page	Evaluation	
			Completed	Comments
*Lucy the Lizard	👄	159	————	————————————
*First Sound Snap 2	👄	160	————	————————————
*Tail Enders 1	✎	161	————	————————————
*Tail Enders 2	✎	162	————	————————————
*Tic-Tac-Toe	✎	163	————	————————————
*Square Up	✎	164	————	————————————
Find the Sounds	✎	165	————	————————————
*Grid Worksheet	✎	166	————	————————————
*Sound Listening	✎	167	————	————————————
*Count Down	✎	168	————	————————————
*How Many Sounds/Letters?	✎	169	————	————————————
*Listen & Match	✎	170	————	————————————
*S at the Start but What's Next?	✎	176	————	————————————
*Blend Blanks	✎	177	————	————————————
*Numberplate Names	✎	178	————	————————————
*Numberplate Nonsense	✎	179	————	————————————
Find the Word	✎	180	————	————————————
Blending				
Blending	👄	182	————	————————————
*Three-Sounded Words A	👄	183	————	————————————
*Three-Sounded Words B	👄	184	————	————————————
A Place for Nonsense	👄	185	————	————————————
*Choose and Change	✎	188	————	————————————
*Visiting the Family	✎	189	————	————————————
*Pop the Bubbles	👄	192	————	————————————
*Blast Off 1	👄	193	————	————————————
*Blast Off 2	👄	194	————	————————————
*Add a Tail	✎	195	————	————————————
*Head-Ons	✎	196	————	————————————
*Flight Path	✎	197	————	————————————
*Blend Bingo	✎	198	————	————————————
Manipulation				
Sound Deletion	👄	202	————	————————————
*Change	✎	205	————	————————————
*Letter Tricks 1	✎	206	————	————————————
*Jumbled Words	✎	207	————	————————————
*Letter Wheels	✎	208	————	————————————
*Letter Tricks 2	✎	209	————	————————————
*Letter Tricks 3	✎	210	————	————————————
*More Jumbled Words	✎	211	————	————————————
*Tricky Triangles	✎	212	————	————————————
*Brainstorming	✎	213	————	————————————
*Real or Unreal	✎	214	————	————————————
*Be A Detective	✎	215	————	————————————
Metalinguistic Trivia 1	👄	216	————	————————————
Metalinguistic Trivia 2	👄	217	————	————————————
Metalinguistic Trivia 3	👄	217	————	————————————

Before You Begin

In this section you will find informal **Phonological Awareness Screening Tests** — one for a teacher and one for a child.

- In the case of **children**, the screening test will help the teacher decide where to begin and which activities to choose for the child. Alternatively, teachers can use the screening test as an observation sheet when working with students individually or in small groups.
  Note: Teachers may find this test more helpful if they are already familiar with the students and their knowledge of language.

- For the **teachers**, the test will give an indication of their own knowledge of sounds and therefore their readiness to embark on these activities with children.

Child Screening for Phonological Awareness

• •

(Teacher presents this test orally to the child)

1 What sound does your name start with?
For example: Michael — 'mmm'.

....

If the child replies with the letter name **M**, confirm that this is the correct letter when his name is written but encourage attention to the sound. If still unsuccessful repeat the name slowly and demonstrate isolating the first sound.

Repeat this process using a friend's name. For example: **Sally** — What sound does her name start with?

If the child's name begins with a vowel, use the child's surname or the name of another family member or friend.

2 Do you know another word that starts with this sound?

....

3 What is the first sound in these words?

sun ☐   party ☐   mummy ☐   fish ☐   gorilla ☐

4 Do these words start with the same sound?

fill   fat   ☐   mouse   two   ☐

bed   boy   ☐   ship   shine   ☐

5 Tell me a word that starts with the sound . . .

't' ....   'n' ....   's' ....

'p' ....   'f' ....   'm' ....

6 Rhyme identification
Some words sound nearly the same — **'rat'**, **'fat'**.
rat and **fat** rhyme because they end the same way. Listen again —
rat, fat.
Do these words rhyme/end the same way?

man	pan	☐		book	head	☐
ball	fall	☐		sock	send	☐
but	hut	☐		rake	make	☐
fight	fine	☐		leap	creep	☐

7 Tell me a word that rhymes with . . .

cat

run

nose

ship

Note:
- Children who cope well with all the tasks are ready to proceed with activities.
- Children who manage tasks 4 and 6 but who find other areas difficult have developed some sensitivity to sound but will require demonstration and explanation beginning with the **What's In A Sound?** section.
- Children who cannot manage any of the tasks will need more explicit instruction, perhaps in a one-to-one relationship, within a program stimulating overall language development.
- Poor performance **may** be indicative of a general language delay or possible hearing impairment and should be investigated further.

Teacher Screening for Phonological Awareness

1 How many *syllables* in each of the following words?

animal	☐	caution	☐	
hastily	☐	catalyst	☐	
revolution	☐	crustacean	☐	
invincible	☐	inconceivable	☐	
stealthily	☐	fortunate	☐	

10

2 How many *sounds* (not letters) in each of the following words?

flag	☐	scone	☐	
rust	☐	clump	☐	
change	☐	straight	☐	
chemist	☐	hiccup	☐	
thought	☐	instrument	☐	

10

3 What is the *second sound* (not second letter) in the following words?

bride	☐	whim	☐	
scream	☐	bought	☐	
queen	☐	thrive	☐	

6

4 What is the *last sound* (not last letter) in the following words?

laugh ☐   though ☐

giraffe ☐   sofa ☐

crisp ☐   arrange ☐

                                        6

5 Join the *rhyming pairs* of words.

stuff   basin   bubble

hasten   some   enough

double   zipper   numb

zither

                                        4

6 Join the words that *begin with the same sound*.

cholera   knave   gentle

pneumonia   chauvinist   quiet

shoal   joke   chef

                                        4

                        TOTAL SCORE   40

Answers

• •

Teacher Phonological Awareness Screening

1 3   2
   3   3
   4   3
   4   5
   3   3

2 4   4
   4   5
   4   5
   6   5
   3   10

3 'r'   'i' as in **i**nk
   'c'   'o'
   'w'   'r'

4 'f'   'o' as in t**oe**
   'f'   'uh' as in **a**ppear
   'p'   'j' as in **j**am

5 stuff — enough
   some — numb
   hasten — basin
   double — bubble

6 cholera — quiet
   chef — chauvinist — shoal
   joke — gentle
   knave — pneumonia

How did you rate?

37+   Well done! Now enjoy the activities with the children.

34–37   Look over your errors — if you understand your confusions proceed with caution.

below 34 You may need to concentrate on improving your own sound awareness before leading children in the activities in this book. Improve your score by reading the **What's In A Sound?** section of this book.

What's In A Sound?

It is wise to spend some time helping children become aware of **where** and **how** speech sounds are made, before proceeding to listening activities.

- **Children** can be encouraged to explore their own '**sound makers**' — lips, tongue, teeth and so on. They can meet the **Mr Mouth** puppet, discover similarities between sounds, and even learn some hand signs for sounds.

- **Adults** will gain information about sounds — where in the mouth and how they are produced, the contrast between voiced and unvoiced sounds, the special properties of vowels. This will assist them in presenting sounds and sound activities in an appropriate sequence.

Sound Makers

• •

Sounds of speech are made in the mouth. While this seems obvious to adults, children are not always aware of how they make speech sounds.

This is quite understandable. When children speak they do not have to pay attention to individual sounds and how they are made — they are intent on getting their meaning across to the listener. During the process of learning to read and spell children are required to focus on individual sounds; to find them within the continuous stream of sound in words and then associate them with written letters.

By introducing the parts of the mouth area that are used to produce speech sounds — the **'sound makers'** — you are preparing children to give their conscious attention to individual sounds.

Talk about **The 'Sound Makers'** while using the puppet-like **Mr Mouth** (p. 16) and during the cleaning of **Mr Tongue's House** (p. 17).

Activity Ideas

• Use a **mirror**. Have a supply of hand mirrors for children to share. A large mirror fixed to a wall is also helpful. Children can see what their lips and tongue are doing and identify the various **'Sound Makers'**.

  Can they see their tonsils?
  What happens when they say **'ah'**?
  Who can reach their nose with the tip of their tongue?

• Use a **flashlight** to aid exploration!

• **Explore** the range and variety of movements of lips and tongue. Think of words to describe some of the movements, such as rolling, folding, pointing, smacking, pursing.

• Adapt **'Simon Says'** or the **Copy Cat** game (see page 124) to encourage accurate imitation of the movement and positioning of the **'Sound Makers'**.

Note: The following activities may not be useful for all the students in your class, but may be useful for those experiencing language delay or articulation problems.

The 'Sound Makers'
lips — top and bottom
tongue — front (including tip) and back
teeth — top and bottom
roof of mouth — front: hard palate or 'ridge'
                       — back: soft palate including uvular
voice box or larynx — in the throat
lungs — this is the source of the airstream
nose — some sounds use the nose rather than the mouth for their resonating chamber

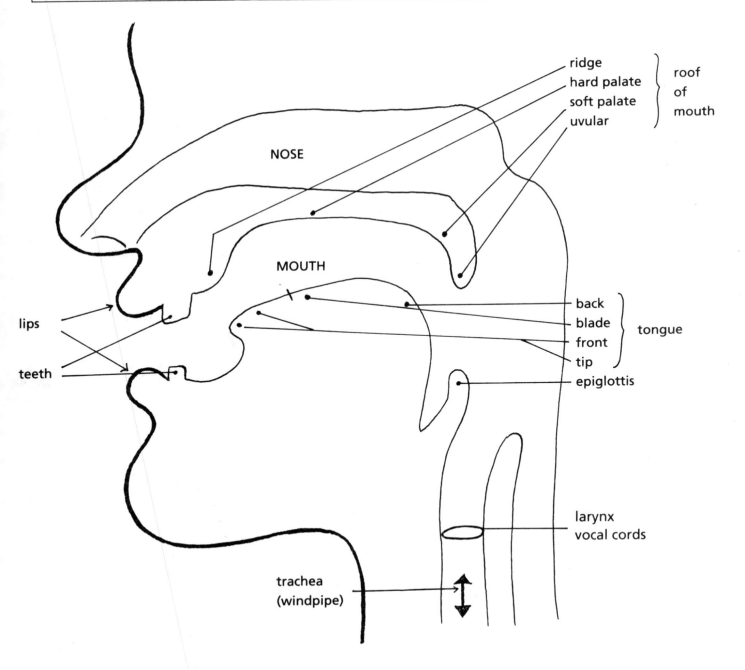

Mr Mouth

• •

Many children need to be taught about sounds before they can easily 'find' them in their own speech.

A **mirror** is useful. Children can look and see what their lips and tongue are doing when they make a particular sound or say a word.

Mr Mouth will help in a similar way. Young children enjoy the puppet-like nature and quickly learn that it represents a time for sound discovery.

It is easily made —

an opened-out wire coat hanger

onto which is threaded and sewn . . .

LIPS (red pantyhose material stuffed with wadding)

onto which is stapled or sewn . . .

TEETH (cardboard or white felt)

TONGUE (thick, pink material such as corduroy, like an oven mitt)

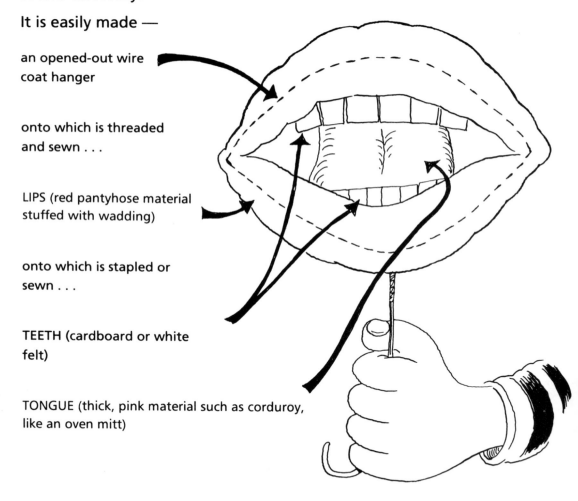

Mr Tongue's House

A game to promote awareness of the '**sound makers**' and the movements involved in speech–sound production.

Suggested story	Action
Mr Tongue lives inside his house.	point to mouth
His front door bell works like this — ring it and see if he is home.	lips together '**mmm**' (or variations)
Mr Tongue opens the front door and comes out onto the front step.	open mouth tongue touches bottom lip
Perhaps he will wave to you.	tongue wiggles
Mr Tongue likes to keep busy cleaning his house. Sometimes he sings while he works.	'**la**' '**la**' '**la**'
Can you hear the vacuum cleaner?	'**nnn**'
After lunch he puts on the dishwasher.	'**sh**' '**sh**' '**sh**'
Later, he chops some wood for the fire.	'**ch**' '**ch**' '**ch**'
Mr Tongue has bought some pictures — he wants to hang them on the walls: – at the front of the house – at the back of the house	'**t**' '**t**' '**t**' (or '**d**' '**d**' '**d**') '**k**' '**k**' '**k**' (or '**g**' '**g**' '**g**')
Mr Tongue notices that his windows are dirty. Can you help him clean them?	run tongue along top teeth — inside and out — then the bottom
Mr Tongue has some flowers by the front door — he stands just outside the front door and waters them every day.	'**th**' '**th**' '**th**'
He also sweeps the leaves from the door step.	'**f**' '**f**' '**f**'
One day Mr Tongue decides to paint the inside of his house — the walls, one side, then the other — and the ceiling.	move tongue along inside surface of cheeks and roof of mouth
Oh no! A fly has got in and might stick to the wet paint. Mr Tongue has to chase the fly from room to room.	tongue moves quickly e.g. behind front teeth inside cheek to touch back teeth
Mr Tongue is now very tired. He goes to bed. Can you hear him snoring? Good night!	tongue rests in mouth '**z**' '**z**' '**z**'

Speech Sounds

There are three main ways in which speech sounds can differ. Ask:

1 **Where** is the sound made?
2 **How** is the sound made?
3 Is the sound **voiced** or **unvoiced?**

(See diagram on page 15)

Knowledge gained in these areas will clarify why some sounds are easily confused.

Where?

Compare where sounds are made. Encourage children to discover differences between, for example:

'f' and **'m'**	**'b'** and **'d'**
't' and **'k'**	**'l'** and **'p'**

How?

Sounds can be placed into broad groups according to how they are made.

'popping' sounds — **'p'   'b'   't'   'd'   'k'   'g'**

'long' sounds — **'f'   'v'   's'   'z'   'sh'   'th'   'l'   'r'**

'nosey' sounds — **'m'   'n'   'ng'**

'combination' sounds — sounds made by closely blending two individual sounds. **'ch'** = **'t'** plus **'sh'** **'j'** = **'d'** plus **'zh'** (as in **measure**)

Demonstrate the differences.

For example:

- How long can one **'p'** sound keep coming out of your mouth?
- Say **'sh'** for as long as you can.
- What happens if you block your nose while saying **'m'**?

Choose a sound and ask questions like 'Is it a long or a "popping" sound?' or 'Does the sound come out your mouth or your nose?'

Voiced or whispered?

Some pairs of sounds are very similar and differ only according to whether or not voice is used — that is, whether or not the vocal cords vibrate during the production of the sound.

NO VOICE (Whispered)	'p' 't' 'k' 's' 'f' 'sh' 'ch' 'th' as in thin
VOICE	'b' 'd' 'g' 'z' 'v' 'zh' as in measure 'j' 'th' as in this

Children, understandably, often confuse the sounds in such pairs when listening and spelling.

Note: It will assist children greatly if you always make the whispered sounds without voice so that the contrast with its voiced 'partner' is emphasized.

For example: the first sound in pig is **'p'** not **'puh'**, (**'puh'** uses voice). You will find the correct way if you isolate the **'p'** on the end of the word 'shop' — say **'p'** by itself, in the same way you say **'p'** at the end of 'shop'.

Helpful hints
Hold a tissue in front of your face as you make each sound in the pairs **'p'/'b'**, **'t'/'d'**, **'k'/'g'**. The whispered sound makes the tissue waver much more!
For **'s'/'z'**, **'f'/'v'**, **'sh'/'zh'** and **'ch'/'j'** pairs — place fingers on front of throat. Feel the vibrations from the larynx during the voiced sounds.

Choose a sound from the no voice–voice table above and ask 'Is it noisy or whispered?'

Speech Sounds

1 WHERE

	both lips	lips & teeth	teeth	ridge	hard palate	soft palate	throat
		← lips teeth →		← roof of mouth →			throat
'popping'	'p' 'b'			't' 'd'		'c' 'k' 'g'	
'long'		'f' 'v'	'th' 'th' as in as in thin this	's' 'z' 'r'	'sh'		
				'ch' 'j'			
'nosey'	'm'			'n'		'ng'	
				'l'			'h'
	'w'					'y'	

2 HOW

3 VOICE

(Unvoiced sound is in left of box.

Voiced sound is in right of box.)

20

Articulation Errors

• •

Sounds acquired in speech at later stages in development, like **'th'**, **'r'** and **'l'**, may not be correctly articulated. Other sounds may also be incorrectly made. For example:

't' for **'k'** as in **tat** for **cat**

'th' for **'s'** as in **theat** for **seat**

It may be tempting to avoid listening activities using these sounds, however, if you go through the **'Sound Maker'** activities (see page 14) and talk about where and how the particular sound is made and then compare it with the sound it is confused with, you may be surprised! The extra information gained by the child may be sufficient to assist him/her to correct the error. For example:

't' — tongue tip taps on the ridge (the roof of the mouth just behind the top teeth)

'k' — back of tongue taps on back of roof of mouth

Say:	**'t'**	**'k'**	**'t'**	**'k'**
	tar	car	tar	car
	tea	key	tea	key

Which Sounds First?

• •

When progressing to sound analysis tasks and establishing links between sounds and letters, it is important to consider which sounds will be easier for the child to 'find'.

In general, sounds that are easier to **see** and **feel** when they are made and those which have very **distinctive auditory characteristics** are easier to 'find' in words.

Easier:	**More difficult:**
'm' 'f' 's' 'n' 'v' 'z' 'h' 'w'	'l' 'r' 'th'

Separate the introduction of similar sounds.
For example: **'m'/'n'   'f'/'v'   's'/'z'**

You will notice that the above sounds are from the 'long group' — (see **Speech Sounds** table page 20) — they can be elongated either in isolation or in words which will assist children's identification.
For example: **zzzzz**oo — **z**oo

ru**nnnn** — run

The 'popping' sounds, particularly those made without voice (**'p'**, **'t'**, **'k'**) are not as easy to isolate at the front of words as the 'long' sounds. (Because of their short 'popping' nature they merge very quickly with the vowel following them.)

'p', **'t'** and **'k'** — may be easier to 'find' at the end of words.

'b', **'d'** and **'g'** — are the voiced 'partners' and may be difficult to identify at the end of words.

For example: 'What is the last sound in re**d**?' Children may repeat the word in a whispered voice which causes the **'d'** to closely resemble a **'t'**.

Note: When introducing the letter–sound links you also should consider which letters look alike and introduce them well apart.
For example: **'h' / 'n'**

'y' / 'g'

A useful system of hand signs exists representing where and how in the mouth each sound is made. This system is called **Cued Articulation** and was devised by Speech Pathologist, Jane Passey. (*Cued Articulation and Cued Vowels*, Jane Passey, ACER 1990.)

The Auditory Discrimination in Depth Program by C. and P. Lindamood also has a systematic way of presenting sounds and their place and manner of production.

But What About the Vowels?

● ●

Vowels are made by the tongue taking up a shape and position in the mouth, thus altering the shape of the space in the mouth.

For some vowels this results in an obvious position of the lips.

For example: **'o'** — as in **o**n

'u' — as in **u**nder

'ee' — as in s**ea**t

For many vowels there is little visible positioning information. Consider mouth shape for the following vowels (in bold print).

sh**or**t	n**igh**t
d**ir**t	l**au**gh
n**oi**se	m**a**k**e**

With vowels there are no contact points between the **'sound makers'** so children can not 'feel' them as easily as they can the consonants.

When linking short vowels (**'a' 'e' 'i' 'o' 'u'**) to their corresponding letters, diagrammatic information about that letter's lip position may be helpful. For example:

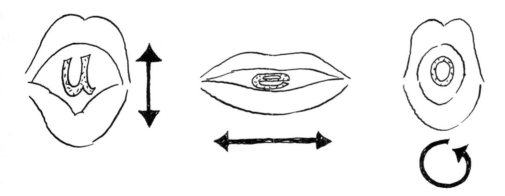

Note: 'u'/'a' 'e'/'i'

These short vowels are often confused — particularly in the middle of words. Children can be assisted with this by carrying out listening activities that use vowels in the initial position of words. Assist also by strengthening the sound-letter links for these vowels.

Sound–Letter Link

Children need to build up sound awareness and
letter knowledge separately.

Links between sounds and letters can then be
firmly established in a way that avoids confusion
and is meaningful to the child.

The activities in this section emphasize the awareness of
sounds, where they come from and their relationship to
letters.

Adults also need to have a clear knowledge of sounds
and letters and be accurate in how they use these terms
with children.

Two 'Baskets' of Knowledge

. . . .

Sounds and Letters

Children need to:
1   be aware of sounds, where they come from and how to 'find' them in words (see the **What's In A Sound?** section and all oral activities), and
2   have a knowledge of the alphabet, recognizing and naming the individual letters and, in time, writing them.

When the knowledge in each 'basket' has been gained children will be ready to link the two 'baskets':
   'the letter is **S** and it usually makes the sound **'sss'** . . .'

The word 'usually' will ensure children realize that there may be exceptions.
   It is wise to use the words **sound** and **letter** very specifically.
* A **letter** is written down and can be seen and named.
* A **sound** is made in the mouth and can be heard.
* Spoken words are made up of sounds, written words are made up of letters.

Why Not Just One Basket?

Some people say that alphabet names are of no use and so they focus only on sounds. Others point out that the many variations of sound–letter correspondence can be confusing. For example: If **a** says '**a**' (as in **a**nt), what about '**a**' in **a**ny, **a**corn, **a**ppeal etc.? These people tend to opt for emphasis on letters.
   Both points of view are valid. However, regardless of the particular focus in a particular class, the child will be exposed to both letter names and sounds at home, on television and so on, and will face the task of sorting out how these names and sounds relate to each other.
   For some children the task is too daunting and they end up with only one basket filled with confused knowledge.
   Consider the letter names for: **g j c f l m n r u y**. When you say their names, the first sound in the name is **not** the sound the letter usually makes. For example: **g** — **'gee'** — **'j'**; **y** — **'wigh'** — **'w'**
   Children must acquire automatic knowledge of letter names and their usual associated sounds.

Alphabet

Sing the Alphabet Song

As you sing:

- Point to the letters on the alphabet chart (p. 29)
- Clap — one clap per letter. This is especially relevant in sections where letters can be said in quick succession. For example:
'elemenopee' L   M   N   O   P
(Some children perceive this as one unit!)
- Use other body movements such as stamping, wiggling and so on.
- Use both upper and lower case alphabet forms (see pp. 29 and 32):

A B C D E F G H I J K...
a b c d e f g h i j k...

Say the Alphabet

- Use ideas from the singing activity above.
- Divide and cut up the alphabet letters (p. 30) into groups of three

abc	def	ghi	jkl

Note: These 'chunks' of the alphabet can then be superimposed on the whole alphabet strips (p.29)

- With a large group, a small group or an individual child, '**say and sort**' to reassemble the alphabet.

Some children will be able to recite the alphabet but will have difficulty recalling the name of some individual letters. The following strategy may help.

abc **def** **ghi**

- Say the alphabet again but increase the time in the 'gap' between the groups of three letters.
- Ask the child to clap hands or blink eyes, etc. before resuming the alphabet sequence.
- Return to the continuous sequence if this is too difficult and put in a very short pause in the 'gaps'.
- Muddle the cards. Can children name them when they are out of order? Can the letters on each card be named in reverse order?

Cut Up the Alphabet

Cut up the alphabet further so that there is **one letter on each card**.

Note: These individual letters of the alphabet can be superimposed onto 3-letter 'chunks' (p. 30) or onto the whole alphabet (p. 29). (Giving each child his/her own set of cards ensures that the child can move on to each activity stage at their own pace.)

- Match individual letters to the alphabet sequence.
- Play 'snap' or 'memory' using two or more sets of alphabet cards. Each time a card is turned over a letter must be named.
- Match lower- and upper-case letters.

Alphabet Strips Lower Case

a b c d e f

g h i j k l

m n o p q r

s t u v w x

y z

Teacher's Notes: See suggested activities (p. 27). All the alphabet strips (pp. 29-32) can be superimposed upon one another.

Alphabet Strips Lower Case

a b c d e f

g h i j k l

m n o p q r

s t u v w x

y z

Teacher's Notes: See suggested activities (p. 27). All the alphabet strips (pp. 29-32) can be superimposed upon one another.

Alphabet Strips Lower Case

a	b	c	d	e	f
g	h	i	j	k	l
m	n	o	p	q	r
s	t	u	v	w	x
y	z				

Teacher's Notes: See suggested activities (p. 27). All the alphabet strips (pp. 29-32) can be superimposed upon one another.

Alphabet Strips Upper Case

A B C D E F

G H I J K L

M N O P Q R

S T U V W X

Y Z

A SOUND WAY: PHONICS ACTIVITIES FOR EARLY LITERACY © 1996. Permission is granted for the purchaser to photocopy this page for non-commercial classroom use. Pembroke Publishers.

Teacher's Notes: See suggested activities (p. 27). All the alphabet strips (pp. 29-32) can be superimposed upon one another.

Personalized Alphabet Charts

● ●

Photocopy the **Personalized Alphabet Charts** (pp. 34 and 35) onto firm paper or card.

- Each child fills in his/her own chart with pictures as different letter–sound links are learned.
- The picture chosen by the child for each letter is the one that **most readily elicits the sound the letter usually represents**.
- The child may choose family members' names, in which case a small photo may be pasted in the appropriate space.
- Discourage less usual sound representations (while at the same time acknowledging that they are correct!). **'g'** for **g**iraffe, **'c'** for **c**eiling.

   Also discourage less common letter representations of the sound. For example: **'f'** **Ph**oebe (But do acknowledge that **ph** can say **'fff'**.)

Note: A similarly personalized chart can be made for digraphs like **'sh'** and long vowels such as **'ee'/'ea'**.

Commercial Alphabet Charts

Before purchasing one of the many commercial alphabet charts or friezes, be sure to check it carefully. Consider the following:

- Are the words chosen appropriate for the children's vocabulary and experience?
- Do the words chosen begin with the **sound** which the letter most commonly represents or just the letter?
- It is better if the word does not begin with a consonant blend.
- Do you want lower- or upper-case letters, or both?
- Are the pictures clear?
- Are two or more pictures easily confused?

These are examples from actual alphabet charts.

- **o** was represented by the number **o**ne
- **g** was represented by **g**iraffe (confusing it with the picture for **j**)
- **u** was represented by the **u**nicorn
- on the same chart: **i** was represented by **i**tchy **w**itchy and **w** by **w**izard. These two had similar illustrations.

Personalized Alphabet Chart

a	h
b	i
c	j
d	k
e	l
f	m
g	n

A SOUND WAY: PHONICS ACTIVITIES FOR EARLY LITERACY © 1996. Permission is granted for the purchaser to photocopy this page for non-commercial classroom use. Pembroke Publishers.

Teacher's Notes: Suggested activities (p. 33).

Personalized Alphabet Chart

v	o
w	p
x	q
y	r
z	s
	t
	u

Teacher's Notes: Suggested activities (p. 33).

Singing Alphabet Cards

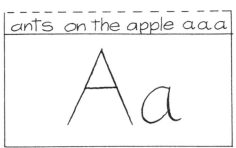

reverse side

- Make large cards as shown above for the letters of the alphabet plus the digraphs **'sh'**, **'ch'**, **'th'**.
- Choose a short phrase — noun + verb or adjective + noun — featuring words that begin with the sound the letter usually represents.
- Draw a clear picture representing the phrase.
- Write the phrase as shown above. This section of the card can then fold back.
- Write upper- and lower-case letters on the reverse of this card.
- Sing the phrase with the children to the tune of 'Skip to my Lou my darling'.
  For example: 'Ants on the apple — **a a a** (repeat 3 times)
  Skip to my Lou my darling!'

Some suggestions for singing alphabet cards.

a	ants on the apple	**k**	kings kicking	**u**	ugly uncles
b	balls bouncing	**l**	licking lollypops	**v**	visiting valentines
c	camels coughing	**m**	monkeys munching	**w**	wild wolves
d	dizzy dinosaurs	**n**	number nine	**x**	ox on a box
e	empty eggs	**o**	orange octupuses	**y**	yellow yachts
f	funny fish	**p**	pink panthers	**z**	zebras zigzag
g	gorillas gardening	**q**	queens quarrelling	**sh**	sharks in the shower
h	helicopters hovering	**r**	rusty robots	**ch**	chattering children
i	itchy insects	**s**	sausages sizzling	**th**	thumbs thinking
j	jumping jellybeans	**t**	tiny teddies		

Use these cards to:

- promote awareness of a particular sound.
- link the sound with the letter.
- practise writing the letter for this sound.
- match words said with words written.

Note: Do the same with children's names.
For example: **T**ina's **t**apping

Alphabet Flash Cards

Photocopy the alphabet cards on the following three pages and make flash cards for use with either a box of objects or picture cards. See **Rhyming Snap** (p. 88), **Odd Man Out** (p. 101), and **Sound Bucket Game** (p. 123).

Choose letters that are appropriate for the children's current level of knowledge. Vowels are often more difficult for children to isolate and so could be left until after sound–letter links are established with several consonants.

Alternatives

- Hold up a flash card and the child:
  - says the sound . . . **or**
  - selects an object or picture that begins with the corresponding sound . . . **or**
  - says the letter name and its corresponding sound.

- Say the sound and the child:
  - writes the letter on the chalkboard . . . **or**
  - finds the correct letter from the pile . . . **or**
  - finds the correct letter in their own writing assignments.

- The child 'finds' the initial sound of a given word or picture and:
  - matches it with the correct letter . . . **or**
  - writes the correct letter.

Alphabet Flash Cards

a   b   c

d   e   f

g   h   i

Teacher's Notes: Suggested activities (p. 37).

Alphabet Flash Cards

j	k	l
m	n	o
p	q	r

Teacher's Notes: Suggested activities (p. 37).

Alphabet Flash Cards

s	t	u
v	w	x
y	z	

Teacher's Notes: Suggested activities (p. 37).

Flips

Flips are designed to prompt the child to link sounds and letters.

Assemble a Flip chart by photocopying the template (p. 42), cutting out the large rectangle, cutting on the dotted lines and folding the small sections to make flaps.

Problem or new letter–sound combinations are represented as in the diagram below.

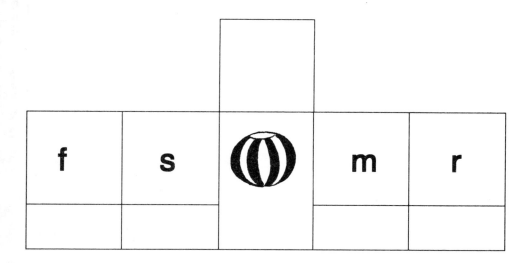

A picture (or photo) is selected by the child. This picture begins with the sound represented by the letter on the flip chart, for example: **apple** for **'a'**, and is drawn (preferably by the child) in the space under the flap so that it will not be visible when the flap is down.

When all **flaps are up** children can check their letter–sound links by saying the name of each picture, finding the initial sound and writing the corresponding letter. Return the flap to check result.

Similarly when **flaps are down** children look at the letter and say the sound — looking at their prompt picture if necessary. Children will learn to prompt themselves and eventually establish automatic sound–letter links.

Flips

fold

A SOUND WAY: PHONICS ACTIVITIES FOR EARLY LITERACY © 1996. Permission is granted for the purchaser to photocopy this page for non-commercial classroom use. Pembroke Publishers.

Teacher's Notes: Copy page, paste onto heavy card, cut on dotted lines and fold flaps.
See also: Instructions and activity ideas (p. 41).

Individual Short Vowel Cards

fold

	a
	e
	i
	o
	u

Teacher's Notes: Use these as flip cards or cut them up for individual vowel study.
See also: **Flips** (p. 41) and **But What About the Vowels?** (p. 23).

Sound Check

• •

Directions for game board (p. 45).

Game One

The teacher calls out a sound and the child finds the corresponding letter on their game board, and covers this letter with a token. Play continues until all letters are covered.

Game Two

This is a game for two players who have made some sound–letter links, but need practice.

Each player chooses an end of the board and covers the first three letters while saying the sounds for those letters.

For example: **m — 'mm'**, **s — 'sss'**, **b — 'b'**.

The players aim to move all their tokens to the other end of the board by moving one token at a time to an adjacent and 'free' letter square. In order to land on a square, the player must say the sound represented by the letter square.

Game Three

This game is played like Game Two, except the child says the letter name, its sound and a word beginning with that sound when they land on a square.

For example: **k — 'k' — kite**.

Sound Check

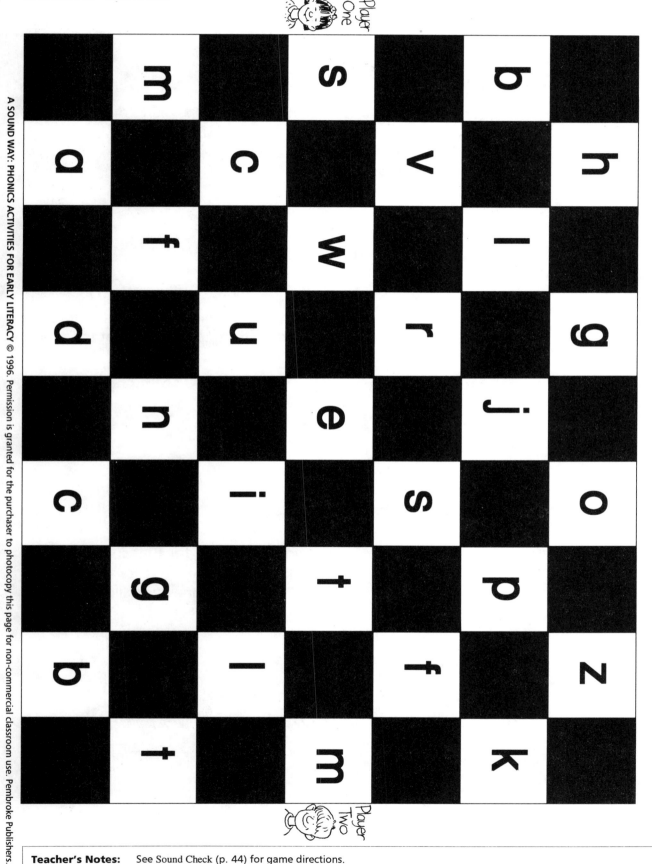

Player One

Player Two

	m		s		b	
a		c		v		h
	f		w		l	
d		u		r		g
	n		e		j	
c		i		s		o
	g		t		p	
b		l		f		z
	t		m		k	

Teacher's Notes: See Sound Check (p. 44) for game directions.

Whose Name Game

• Children are given charts of blank squares (or asked to draw and number them).
The number of squares should correspond to the number of letters in a chosen child's name.
For example:

1	2	3	4	5	6

S   o   p   h   i   e

• Do not tell the children whose name has been chosen and make them wait until all clues are given before indicating that they have discovered the answer.

• Indicate which number square the clue is for — either going from **1** in a left-to-right sequence — or make the task harder by mixing up the order.

Clues

Use any of these clues, or a combination.
• Name a letter and have children write it.
• Give a sound. Children then write the letter for that sound.
• Give a word. Children then work out what the word starts with and write the letter for that sound. This involves analysis skills (pp. 121-180).

Word Awareness

The activities in this section help children to identify words within sentences.

When speaking, children do not usually concentrate on individual words, but this is useful when they are learning to read.

In these activities, children will develop an awareness of words in spoken and written sentences and understand that word order has an effect on sentence meaning.

Compound words are introduced to encourage the child to look within the word for meaningful parts. This is a strategy which children will find helpful when spelling larger words.

Breaking Up A Sentence

- Choose sentences of increasing length (see sentence list on p. 49).

- Say the sentence — children repeat it out loud.

- Children then identify the words in the sentence. Some children may be ready to discover the actual number of words, but it is more important that **word boundaries** are recognized.

- Let the children jump, clap or tap on a desk as they discover each word.

- Visual representation is also helpful. Blocks, counters, tags from bread packets etc. can be moved as the sentence is said. Similarly, lines can be marked on the paper.

  For example, while saying '**Oranges are very juicy**' mark — — — —.

  Children will find it easier to count the words in the sentence using this visual representation.

- Write down the chosen sentence and point to each word as children repeat the sentence out loud.

- Smaller 'fill-in' words such as articles, conjunctions, prepositions and pronouns (**the, a, so, but, to, on, her, he** etc.) will be harder to identify as words than more concrete nouns and verbs, so begin with shorter, simpler sentences.

- Similarly, sentence structures not yet in the child's oral language repertoire will be difficult for the child to repeat and identify word boundaries accurately. For example:

  '**Sally was taken to school by her Mother's friend**' becomes '**Mum's friend taked Sally to school**'!

- A more difficult activity is to choose a familiar story book for sentence examples or ask children to suggest their own sentences for breaking up.

Sentence list for 'Breaking Up a Sentence'

Catch it.	May I have a turn?	It is nearly time to go home.
Sit down.	Rainy days are fun.	Whose bag is that over there?
Go away.	Where is my book?	We can learn a lot from books.
I like dogs.	Big dogs jump high.	Will the show be open on Friday?
Come here.	I built a huge bridge.	Candies are not good for our teeth.
Give me two.	Mac is milking the cow.	Why do giraffes have long necks?
Please eat now.	Mr Brown is my teacher.	The big truck slid on the wet road.
Sally runs fast.	I just heard the bell ring.	Bears like to hide and sleep in winter.
He loves to skip.	When can Peter play tennis?	The furry ginger cat drank all the milk.
The lion is angry.	She will let you play cards.	I need my umbrella because it might rain.
We eat spicy food.	The little mice are sleeping.	

Breaking Sentences

● ●

- Choose sentences related to a student's 'news' or class theme, then read these aloud to the class.

- Ask the children to represent each word in the sentence with a counter, bead or other token.
  For example:

    Pets — I have a dog. (4)
    The child places four tokens   ●   ●   ●   ●
    My dog barks loudly. (4)
    I have two fish and a rabbit. (7)

    Recreation — I have a big bike. (5)
    We play in the park. (5)
    I like to take Freddy to the park. (8)

- Write a sentence on the chalkboard. Show the children one word as each word is read. Can the children change the sentence by thinking of one new word to replace an old word?
  For example: My sister is **little**. My sister is **naughty**.

    Cross out the old word and write the new one. Recount the words. Has the meaning of the sentence changed?

Rearranging Sentences

- Select a suitable sentence and write it onto flash cards so that each word of the sentence is on a separate card.

- Distribute the flash cards to selected students. The children represent 'their' words. Arrange these 'words' (children) in a row from left to right in front of the class.

- Starting from the left, each child calls out his or her word in turn to say the whole sentence.

- You (or another student) can then rearrange the 'word' order. Does the sentence still make sense?

- This task highlights the function of words within sentences, directionality in reading (i.e. left to right), as well as how sentence meaning alters with changes in word order.
  For example:

  I can jump high.   Can I jump high? I can high jump.

  Sentence Suggestions:
  The boy hit a big ball.
  Please sit down carefully on the chair.
  Tom and Mary have a large dog and a small cat.
  On Saturday we will play with our new toys and our friends.

- Extend the activity by altering the sentences so that they express a negative statement or ask a question.
  For example: The boy did not hit a big ball.
               Did the boy hit a big ball?

What's Left 1?

What is left if I take the **stick** from **broomstick**?

Skill:	Recognizing and deleting the parts of a compound word.
Teacher's Notes:	Using the **What's Left? 1 word list** (p. 53), ask children questions like, 'What is left if I take the **stick** from **broomstick**?' Have children circle their answers. Use **Compound Word Activities** (pp. 58-65) for activities to be shared with parents or older children.
See also:	**What's Left 2?** (p. 52).
Extension:	Children point to the pictures and create their own compound words, for example, pig-sty, door-knob.

What's Left 2 ?

What is left if I take the **tea** from **teapot**?

Skill:	Recognizing and deleting the parts of a compound word.
Teacher's Notes:	Using the **What's Left 2? word list** (p. 53), ask children questions like, 'What is left if I take the **tea** from **tea**pot? Have children circle their answers. Use **Compound Word Activities** (pp. 58-65) for activities to be shared with parents or older children.
See also:	**What's Left 1?** (p. 51).
Extension:	Children point to the pictures and create their own compound words, for example, pig-sty, door-knob.

What's Left?

Use these words for the activities on pages 51 and 52. The words in parentheses indicate those to be omitted.

What's Left 1? word list
For example:

What is left if I take the **stick** from **broom (stick)**?

rain(bow)	bird(bath)
grass(hopper)	door(step)
star(fish)	moon(light)
foot(ball)	lip(stick)
pig(tail)	sun(shine)

What's Left 2? word list
For example:

What is left if I take the **tea** from **(tea)pot**?

(pan)cake	(bus)stop
(stop)watch	(gold)fish
(tea)spoon	(house)boat
(book)case	(eye)ball
(paint)brush	(sun)hat

Vary What's Left?

Using the activity **What's Left 1?** or **What's Left 2?** or both together, vary the task by creating new words. Remove initial or final word randomly.

ball(room)	(back)door
house(guest)	fish(tank)
(bulls)eye	(movie)star
hat(band)	house(boat)
door(bell)	(hair)brush
house(full)	door(knob)
watch(band)	eye(lid)
(straw)broom	(basket)ball
spoon(ful)	house(work)
(light)house	(tug)boat

Make Your Own Words

sun	case	stick	tie
fan	rain	light	nail
wreck	toe	book	belt
moon	bow	lip	broom
seat	coat	ship	space

Skill:	Creating compound words from picture cues.
Teacher's Notes:	Children cut out the pictures and join them in pairs to make as many compound words as they can. Each picture can be used more than once. This activity requires children to have a sophisticated knowledge of language — do not try with early readers.
See also:	**Compound Word Activities** (pp. 58-65) for activities that can be shared with parents or older children.
Extension:	Children make up nonsense compound words from the pictures and as a class they discuss possible meanings, for example, nail-case.

A SOUND WAY: PHONICS ACTIVITIES FOR EARLY LITERACY © 1996. Permission is granted for the purchaser to photocopy this page for non-commercial classroom use. Pembroke Publishers.

Make Your Own Words Again

ball	'tee'	hand	bell
stand	watch	chair	flower
shell	door	time	egg
arm	band	head	foot
cup	house	hat	mat
stop	pot	bed	path

Skill: Creating compound words from picture cues.
Teacher's Notes: Children cut out the pictures and join them in pairs to make as many compound words as they can. Each picture can be used more than once.
See also: **Compound Word Activities** (pp. 58-65) for activities that can be shared with parents or older children.
Extension: Children make up nonsense compound words from the pictures and as a class they discuss possible meanings, for example, nail-case.

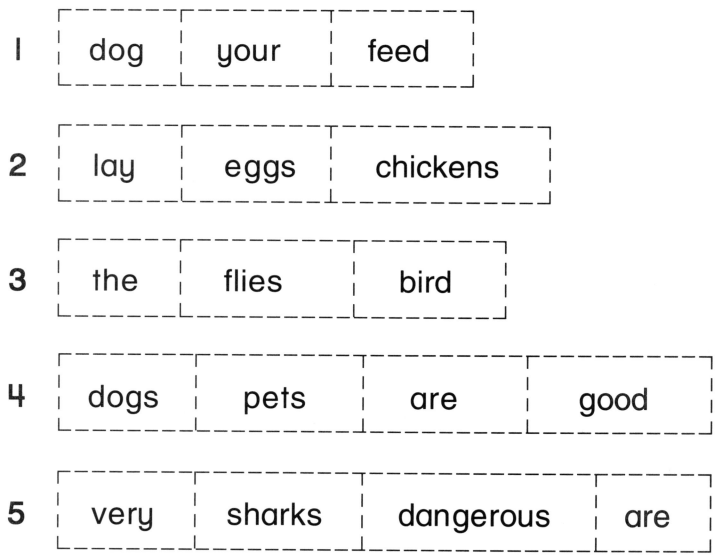

Sentence Cut ups

- Cut up each jumbled sentence into separate words.
- Arrange the words in the correct order to make a sentence.
- Paste them onto a piece of paper.
- Read them.

1 | dog | your | feed |

2 | lay | eggs | chickens |

3 | the | flies | bird |

4 | dogs | pets | are | good |

5 | very | sharks | dangerous | are |

Skill: Arranging written words in a sentence.
Teacher's Notes: This activity's purpose is to identify individual words in sentences and show how placement of words can change sentence meaning.
Extension: Children write their own sentences for a partner to arrange, or they can use sentences from **Breaking Up a Sentence** (p. 49).

A SOUND WAY: PHONICS ACTIVITIES FOR EARLY LITERACY © 1996. Permission is granted for the purchaser to photocopy this page for non-commercial classroom use. Pembroke Publishers.

Build
Build Up
Build Up Sentences

- Rewrite the short sentence as many times as you can, each time adding **one** new word.
- It must make a real sentence at each level.

For example: Dogs bark.
Dogs bark loudly.
Mean dogs bark loudly.
Mean black dogs bark loudly.

1   Boys run.
2   Go away.
3   Winds blow.
4   Let me.
5   Come now.
6   Sit down.
7   Grandpa went.
8   Fill the jug.
9   Sally had a dream.
10 Pigs smell.

Skill:	Expanding a sentence one word at a time, while retaining correct grammar.
Extension:	Do this activity orally as a class or in groups. Which group can make the longest sentence? Be sure to add only one word at a time.

"Go Togethers"

Find the two words that go together to form a compound word. Draw a line to join them. **Football** has been done for you.

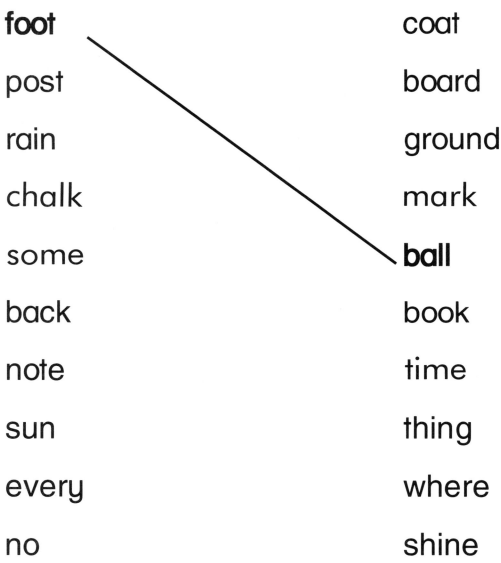

foot	coat
post	board
rain	ground
chalk	mark
some	**ball**
back	book
note	time
sun	thing
every	where
no	shine

A SOUND WAY: PHONICS ACTIVITIES FOR EARLY LITERACY © 1996. Permission is granted for the purchaser to photocopy this page for non-commercial classroom use. Pembroke Publishers.

Skill:	Creating compound words from written cues.
Teacher's Notes:	The following compound word activities illustrate how words can be formed into compound words. This knowledge helps children in spelling compound words.
See also:	**Word Match-Up** (p. 61).
Extension:	Children make a list of other compound words they know to share with the class.

Divide

Draw a line dividing these compound words into two words.
Write the two parts on the lines provided.

e.g. foot|ball football foot ball	postbox
hideout	mailbags
blackberry	tablecloth
livingroom	bookworm
policeman	swimsuit
carpet	toothpaste
handsome	suntan

A SOUND WAY: PHONICS ACTIVITIES FOR EARLY LITERACY © 1996. Permission is granted for the purchaser to photocopy this page for non-commercial classroom use. Pembroke Publishers.

Skill: Dividing compound words into two words.
See also: **Make Your Own Words** (pp. 54-55)
Extension: Choose one part of a compound word and have the class 'brainstorm' for other compound words, for example, tooth(paste) — toothache, toothbrush, toothfairy.

COMPOUND WORDS

Make as many words as you can that begin with these words.
Write them in the box.

e.g. **sun**	sunshine suntan sunscreen sunset sunburn Sunday sunrise sunlight
some	
door	
tooth	
rain	
snow	
back	

Skill:	Writing compound words from a written word.
Extension:	Children use the pictures from **Make Your Own Words** (pp. 54-55) to write as many compound words as they can on the back of this page.

60

Word match-up

Match up these jigsaw pieces to form compound words.

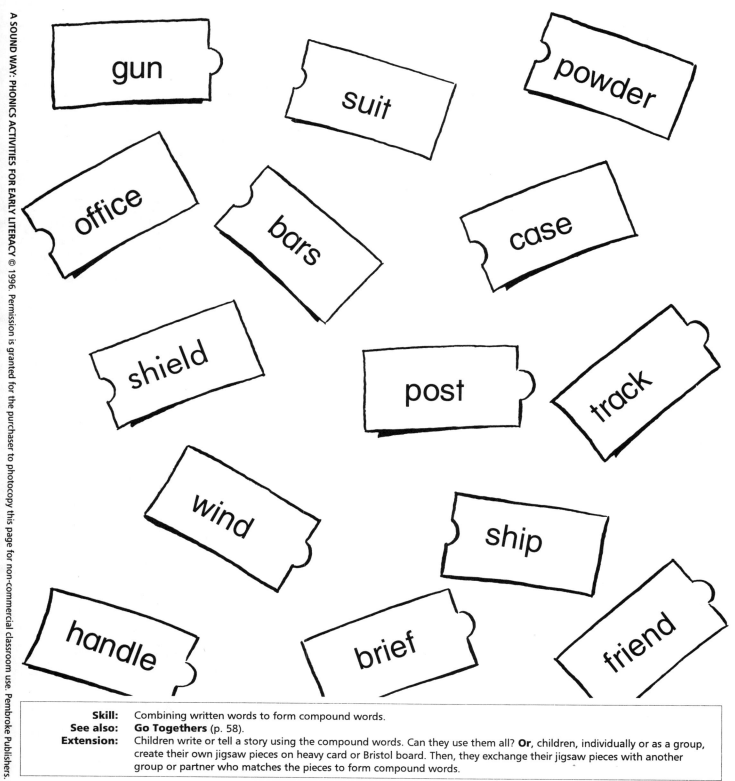

gun

suit

powder

office

bars

case

shield

post

track

wind

ship

handle

brief

friend

Skill: Combining written words to form compound words.
See also: **Go Togethers** (p. 58).
Extension: Children write or tell a story using the compound words. Can they use them all? **Or**, children, individually or as a group, create their own jigsaw pieces on heavy card or Bristol board. Then, they exchange their jigsaw pieces with another group or partner who matches the pieces to form compound words.

Compound Corner and Compound Racetrack

Compound Corner (p. 63)

This is a game for 2–3 players, who take turns to roll dice and move their tokens along the track. The aim is to create compound words from pictorial cues.

Starting on the square with a | key | pictured, players move their token the number of squares shown on the dice. As they turn a corner (i.e. pass a picture square) they must say a compound word starting with the picture illustrated. For example: **key** — **keyhole**.

Depending on the number thrown and their position on the track, a player may be required to say up to four compound words. Encourage alternative answers, for example: **footpath, football, footstool, footman**.

Compound Racetrack (p. 64)

This is similar to the game above except that word stimuli alone are used and players must be flexible in supplying beginning or ending words to make the compound word.
For example: **back**yard and ham**burger**

Refer to compound words often in classroom language tasks, spelling and reading to consolidate learning.

COMPOUND CORNER

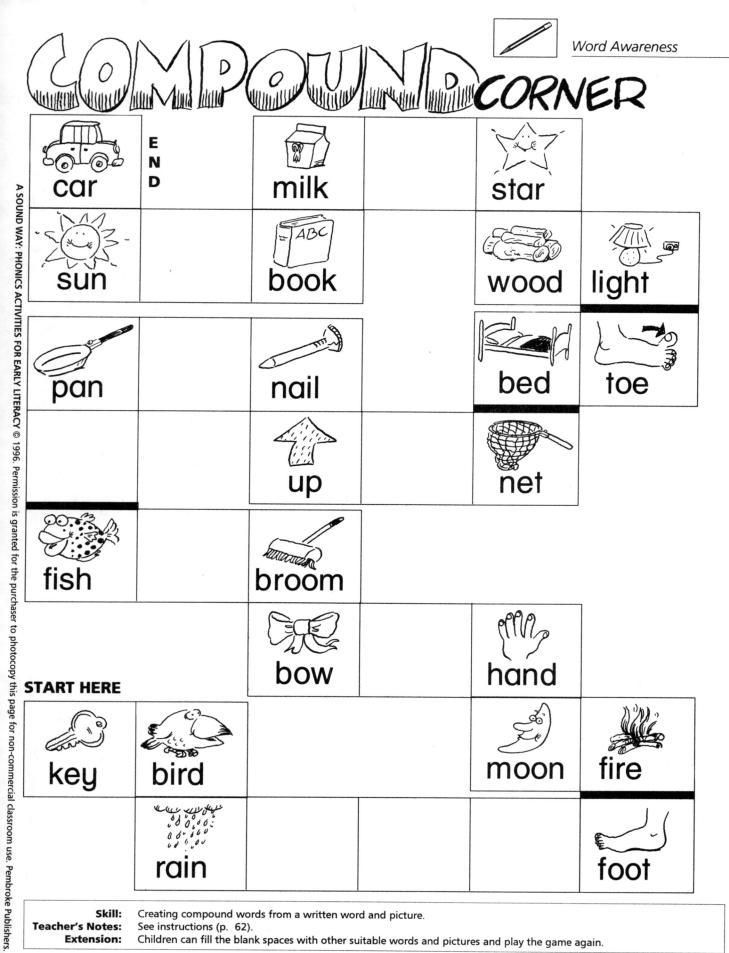

	E N D	milk		star
car				
sun		book	wood	light
pan		nail	bed	toe
		up	net	
fish		broom		
		bow	hand	
key	bird		moon	fire
	rain			foot

START HERE

Skill:	Creating compound words from a written word and picture.
Teacher's Notes:	See instructions (p. 62).
Extension:	Children can fill the blank spaces with other suitable words and pictures and play the game again.

63

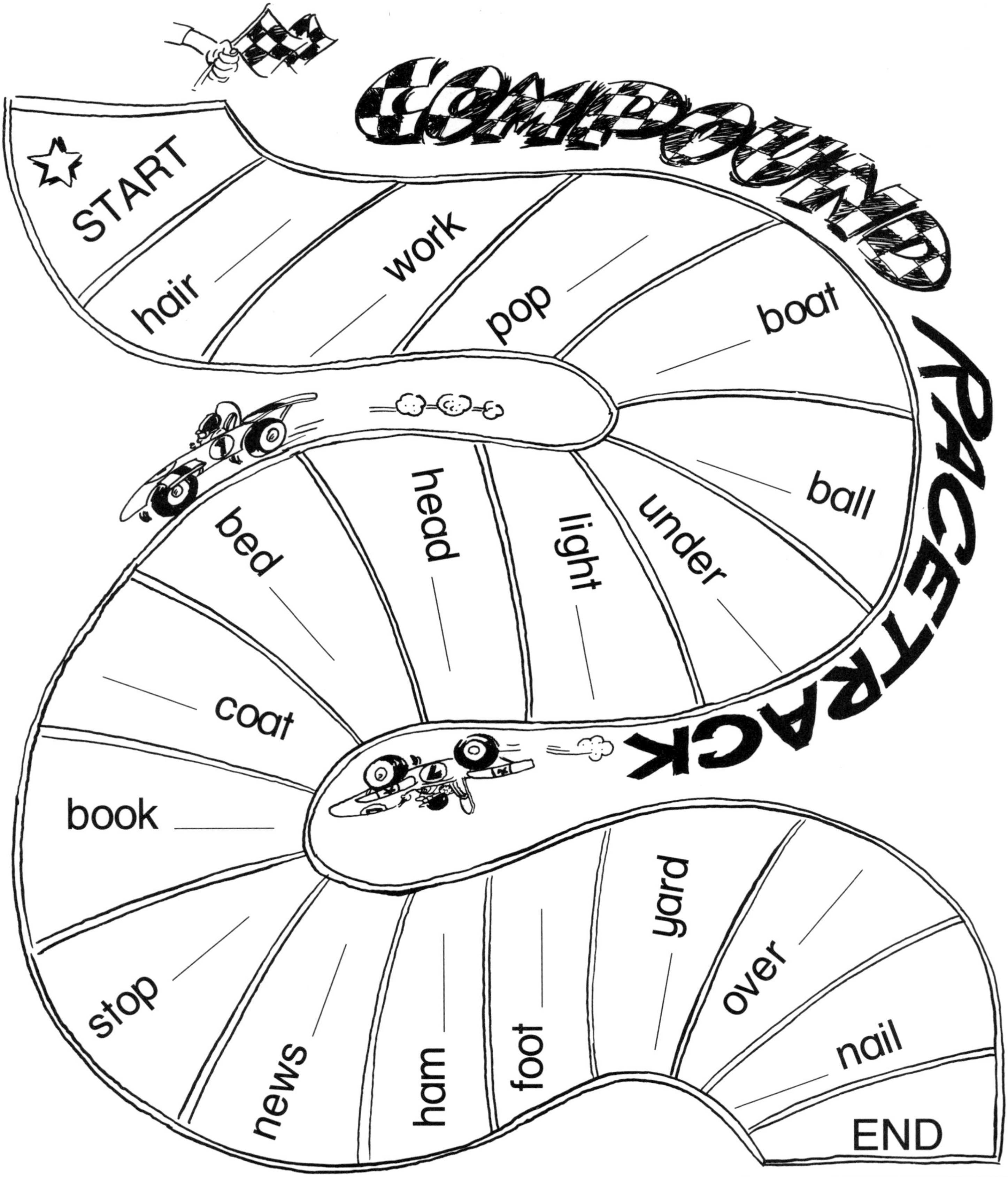

START
★

hair ____

work ____

pop ____

boat ____

ball ____

under ____

light ____

head ____

bed ____

coat ____

book ____

stop ____

news ____

ham ____

foot ____

yard ____

over ____

nail ____

END

COMPOUND RACETRACK

Skill:	Writing or saying compound words when half of the compound has been supplied.
Teacher's Notes:	See instructions (p. 62).
Extension:	Children play the game again and think of different words to write or say.

64

'Two in One' 2

Draw the two parts of the compound word in one picture.

e.g.  handbag

footpath	snowshoe
headlight	milkman
cowboy	pancake
rainbow	bookworm

Skill: Illustrating the two parts of compound words in one picture.
Teacher's Notes: This activity is a challenge for young and old. Children will enjoy sharing it with other family members.
Extension: Using the pictures from **Make Your Own Words** (pp. 54-55), children make up nonsense compound words and try to illustrate them, for example, belt-book. Have a competition for the most novel invention. **Or,** teacher picks compound words from students' own writing and asks them to draw the two parts of the word in one picture.

Syllables

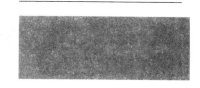

In this section children divide spoken words into syllables or 'beats' — a task which is easier than finding the individual sounds within the words.

In the early activities children are provided with visual representations for the syllables to make the task more concrete. They should also be encouraged to move their body, clap, tap etc., to help them find the syllables as they say the words.

Later, spelling is facilitated by matching syllables found in spoken words to their written equivalents.

Syllables

Syllable Signs

1 ◯

2 ◯ ◯

3 ◯ ◯ ◯

4 ◯ ◯ ◯ ◯

Skill: Identifying the number of syllables in spoken words.
Teacher's Notes: Children cut out the four cards and colour the circles on each card a different colour. These cards can be used with many syllable activities, for example, **Clap and Move to Syllables** (p. 70).
Extension: Children draw pictures of words with 1, 2, 3 and 4 syllables and match these to the syllable signs.

A SOUND WAY: PHONICS ACTIVITIES FOR EARLY LITERACY © 1996. Permission is granted for the purchaser to photocopy this page for non-commercial classroom use. Pembroke Publishers.

Say and Colour

 ●●○○

'trailer'

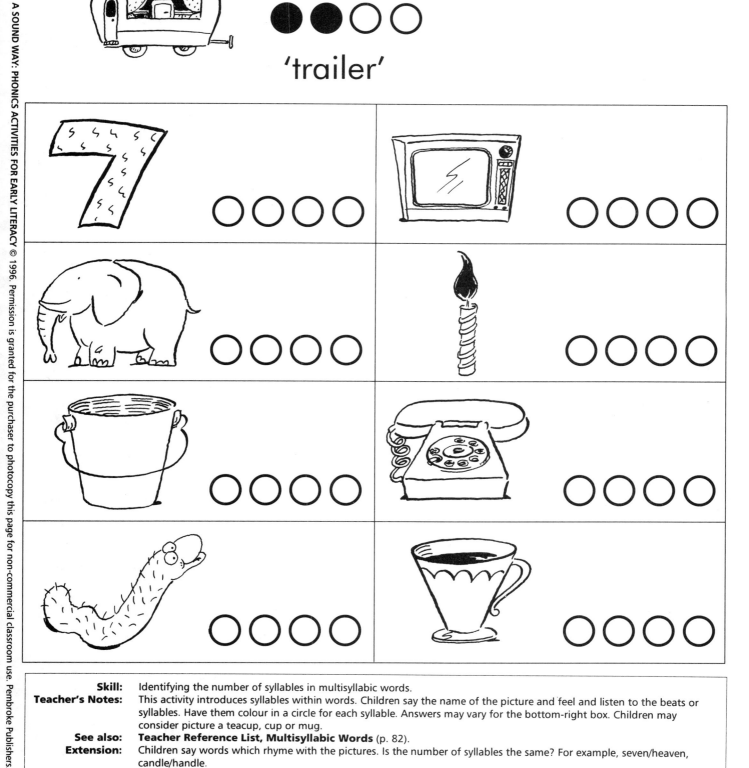

A SOUND WAY: PHONICS ACTIVITIES FOR EARLY LITERACY © 1996. Permission is granted for the purchaser to photocopy this page for non-commercial classroom use. Pembroke Publishers.

Skill:	Identifying the number of syllables in multisyllabic words.
Teacher's Notes:	This activity introduces syllables within words. Children say the name of the picture and feel and listen to the beats or syllables. Have them colour in a circle for each syllable. Answers may vary for the bottom-right box. Children may consider picture a teacup, cup or mug.
See also:	**Teacher Reference List, Multisyllabic Words** (p. 82).
Extension:	Children say words which rhyme with the pictures. Is the number of syllables the same? For example, seven/heaven, candle/handle.

69

Clap and Move to Syllables

The following words have been broken into syllables. Use these words as a fun listening and motor activity. They can also be used in conjunction with the **Syllable Sign Cards** (p. 68).

up (1)

cat-er-pil-lar (4)

ship (1)

car-pet (2)

teach-er (2)

sis-ter (2)

ice-cream (2)

tel-e-vi-sion (4)

im-pos-si-ble (4)

Mon-day (2)

shoe (1)

ro-bot (2)

book (1)

ac-ro-bat (3)

mu-sic (2)

rein-deer (2)

mag-ic (2)

hon-ey (2)

rul-er (2)

mum-my (2)

di-no-saur (3)

sum-mer (2)

sil-ly (2)

pen-cil (2)

milk (1)

tap (1)

hos-pi-tal (3)

kin-der-gar-ten (4)

ted-dy (2)

py-ja-mas (3)

toi-let (2)

lem-on-ade (3)

Chris-to-pher (3)

run-ning (2)

par-ty (2)

bas-ket-ball (3)

su-per-mar-ket (4)

moon (1)

dog (1)

soap (1)

mar-ma-lade (3)

no-one (2)

cof-fee (2)
el-e-phant (3)
ham-bur-ger (3)
doc-tor (2)
fun-ny (2)
cat (1)
tooth-brush (2)
car-a-van (3)
jump (1)
dan-ger (2)
dis-ap-point-ing (4)

phone (1)
um-brel-la (3)
tel-e-phone (3)
air-plane (2)
birth-day (2)
ba-by (2)
al-li-ga-tor (4)
mon-ey (2)
tram-po-line (3)
or-ches-tra (3)

Say a target word. Choose children's names to start with. You can also use the words listed here, or words from children's own life: school name, McDonalds, rollerblades, etc. Ask the children to identify the syllables in the word in any of the following ways:
• clapping
• tapping
• clicking fingers
• nodding their heads
• swivelling their hips
• placing tokens on a chart
• displaying the appropriate Syllable Sign card

Some younger children may find it easier to identify the number of syllables if they associate a syllable (or beat) with an action, such as touching their head, tummy and knees. Then ask them which syllable was related to their knees.

A list of less familiar or more difficult words can be found in the Teacher Reference List of Multisyllabic Words (p. 82).

To extend the activity, segment the words from the list into syllables and ask children to blend them to form whole words. Use a mixture of syllables to make fantasy words. For example: cof-burg-ade, doc-brush, sis-van, di-no-burger, moon-pit-er. What could these words mean?

What's in a Name?

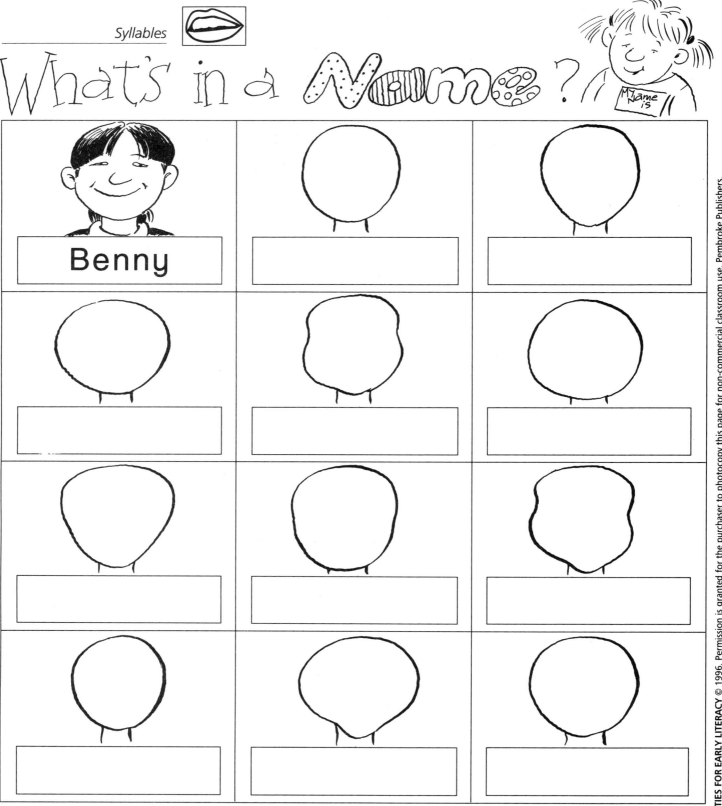

Benny

Skill: Identifying syllables in names.

Teacher's Notes: Children draw faces and think of family or friends' names for them. Children write these names under the picture. Children then cut out the pictures and sort them into piles according to how many syllables are in the names. Ask whether the names have 1, 2, 3, 4 or more syllables. Use **Syllable Signs** (p. 68).

Extension: Children form groups according to the number of syllables in their names. Beginning at the same time, ask all the children to say their names together, while clapping the syllables. Do they all finish at the same time? What happens when other groups say their names at the same time?

Say the names of things you can see in your classroom.
Work out how many syllables are in each name then write the
names in the appropriate boxes.

1 •	2 • • e.g. teacher
3 • • •	4 • • • •
more than 4	

A SOUND WAY: PHONICS ACTIVITIES FOR EARLY LITERACY © 1996. Permission is granted for the purchaser to photocopy this page for non-commercial classroom use. Pembroke Publishers.

Skill:	Categorizing words according to the number of syllables.
Teacher's Notes:	This activity introduces children to multisyllabic words.
Extension:	Children mark on the words where the syllable breaks occur, for example, oc\ta\gon.

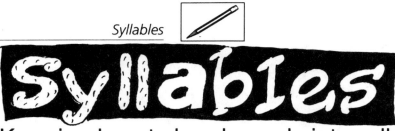

Syllables

Knowing how to break words into syllables can help you read and spell longer words.

Each syllable contains a **vowel**.

im + por + tant = **important**

Break up these words into syllables.

hospital	alligator
caterpillar	machinery
diagonal	disco
information	volcano
adventure	composer
inspection	station
newspaper	mystery
watermelon	advantage

Now choose 3 words and use them in a sentence.

_____

_____

_____

_____

Skill:	Dividing written words into syllables.
Teacher's Notes:	This activity teaches spelling skills by asking children to identify syllables within words. See the activities on pages 75, 76, 78, 79, 80 and 81 also.
Extension:	Children practise **robot talk** dividing every word into syllables, for example, 'My name is Bo-ti-kar. I come from Plan-et Ju-pi-ter.

Long Words Made Simple

Here are some long words which you can break into parts or 'syllables'.

Tap out the syllables.

Write the number of syllables in the box.

For example: **hospital**   hos pi tal   [3]

calendar   ☐   investigation   ☐

freedom   ☐   gingerbread   ☐

traffic   ☐   submarine   ☐

elephant   ☐   seventeen   ☐

government ☐   festival   ☐

important   ☐   disappoint   ☐

invisible   ☐   pencil   ☐

television ☐   available   ☐

alphabet   ☐   caterpillar   ☐

A SOUND WAY: PHONICS ACTIVITIES FOR EARLY LITERACY © 1996. Permission is granted for the purchaser to photocopy this page for non-commercial classroom use. Pembroke Publishers.

Skill: Counting syllables.
See also: **Counting On Frank** (p. 76).
Extension: Children find ten brand names in their cupboards at home or in the supermarket. Write the names down and count the syllables. If each syllable costs 50 cents, how much did it cost you to buy these products?

Counting on Frank

How many syllables in each word?

Tap out the syllables.

Write the number of syllables in the box.

For example: **however** | 3 |

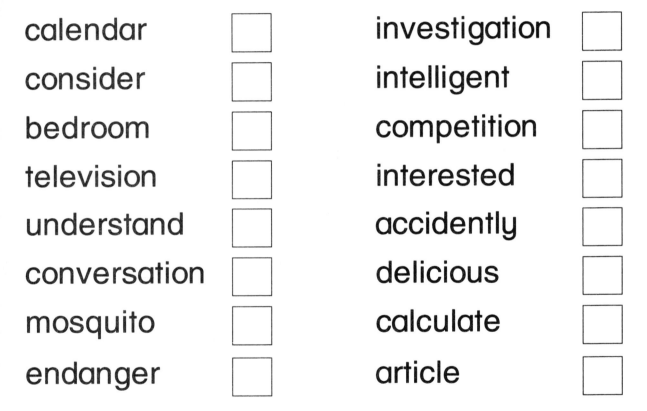

calendar ☐

consider ☐

bedroom ☐

television ☐

understand ☐

conversation ☐

mosquito ☐

endanger ☐

investigation ☐

intelligent ☐

competition ☐

interested ☐

accidently ☐

delicious ☐

calculate ☐

article ☐

A SOUND WAY: PHONICS ACTIVITIES FOR EARLY LITERACY © 1996. Permission is granted for the purchaser to photocopy this page for non-commercial classroom use. Pembroke Publishers.

Skill: Counting syllables.

See also: **Long Words Made Simple** (p. 75).

Extension: Children choose a favourite book and record multisyllabic words or write a class story containing only words of one, two and three syllables.

How many words can you make using these prefixes and syllables? Write them on the lines below. Two have been done.

re	port
de	mote
in	ject
pro	tect
trans	vent
pre	fer

report, remote

_____

_____

_____

Skill:	Matching prefixes and syllables to create real words.
Teacher's Notes:	If children are unfamiliar with prefixes, introduce this activity by explaining that prefixes are a syllable or syllables put at the beginning of another syllable or word to create a word, for example, *dis*rupt, *un*kind.
See also:	**Mixed-Up Syllables** (p. 78) and **Target Practice** (p. 79).
Extension:	Children make a list of other words beginning with the given prefixes, for example, protest, professor.

Mixed-Up Syllables

Make three-syllable words by drawing a line joining a syllable from each of the columns.

For example (**mis-tak-en**).

re	kind	able
un	cus	sion
dis	turn	ness
pre	vent	**en**
con	grate	ed
re	**tak**	ment
mis	cite	ing
ex	tec	ment
un	trast	ful
pro	fresh	tion

Write two words that start with the following prefixes.

tele _____

un _____

re _____

Skill:	Combining written syllables to form words using prefixes and suffixes.
Teacher's Notes:	This activity is well-suited for small group work.
See also:	**Prefix Power** (p. 77).
Extension:	Children use the words — **prevent, transport** and **inject** and add different suffixes from this page. How many words can they make?

Read the syllables in the direction of the arrows to discover target words.

For example: **su → per → mar → ket**

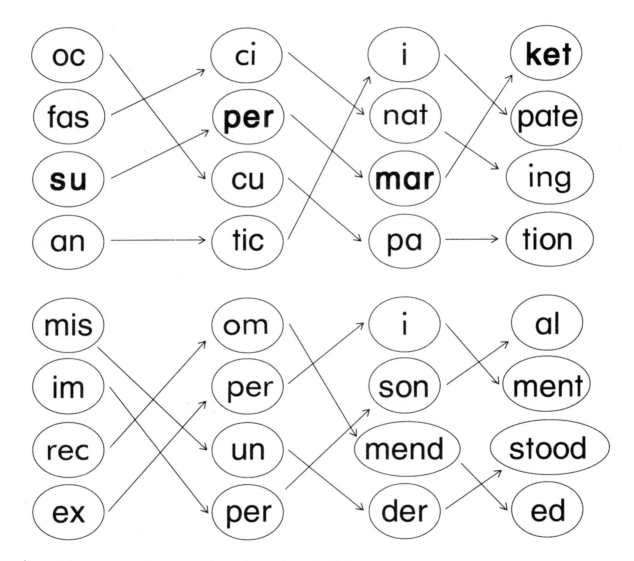

Write the words on the back of this page.

A SOUND WAY: PHONICS ACTIVITIES FOR EARLY LITERACY © 1996. Permission is granted for the purchaser to photocopy this page for non-commercial classroom use. Pembroke Publishers.

Skill:	Blending written syllables.
See also:	**Multisyllabic Word List** (p. 82) and **Prefix Power** (p. 77).

Syllables

SYLLABLE CLUES

Read the clue and write the answer breaking it into syllables. Each box should contain one syllable.

e.g. Large African animal =

el	e	phant

Opposite of forget =

A place to keep things cold =

A large fire-breathing creature in legends =

A place where sick people go =

A house on wheels =

Magic word =

Unable to be seen =

A place to study when you leave high school =

Skill:	Solving a puzzle using syllables.
Teacher's Notes:	Answers: re-mem-ber, re-frig-er-a-tor, dra-gon, hos-pi-tal, trail-er, ab-ra-ca-dab-ra, in-vis-i-ble, u-niv-er-sity
See also:	**Multisyllabic Word List** (p. 82).
Extension:	Each child is given a list of eight words from the **Teacher Reference List of Multisyllabic words** (p. 82) and creates a syllable clue activity for a partner.

Using reading material, classroom discussion or your own written work, write long words in the space below.

Find the word with the **most letters**.

Find the word with the **most syllables**.

Are they the same word?

Word with the most letters	Word with the most syllables

Skill: Counting syllables and letters in words.
Extension: Count the syllables in **supercalafragalisticexpialidocious.**

Teacher Reference List
Multisyllabic Words

2	3	4	5
swimming	coconut	operation	examination
movie	extremely	obviously	international
relax	oxygen	television	creativity
enter	potatoes	geography	university
exit	hexagon	disappointed	extraordinary
textbook	clarinet	misunderstood	investigated
because	torpedo	disqualified	ophthalmologist
monkey	stereo	recommended	hypothetical
cover	volcano	experiment	alphabetical
wooden	mystery	circumference	consideration
racing	favourite	supermarket	congratulations
himself	discussion	supersonic	experimental
parent	violin	extravagant	communication
delay	disagree	ridiculous	geographical
flavour	explosion	illustration	civilization
neighbour	disappear	machinery	administration
pigeon	musician	horizontal	intellectual
distance	disobey	alligator	opportunity
northern	prevention	collapsible	systematical
disco	enemy	Australia	accommodation
chalet	animal	America	anniversary
certain	hospital	regulation	multiplication
before	tomato	astrology	representative
Sunday	certainly	calculator	individual
elbow	telephone	superficial	refrigerator
picture	different	information	intermediate
ruler	genuine	decoration	supplementary
number	instruction	electronic	association
teacher	dinosaur	presentation	chronological
parcel	moccasin	calligraphy	antibiotic
letter	carpenter	adventurous	co-ordination
wiggle	detective	unusual	disagreeable
around	afternoon	variations	astronomical
seven	microwave	interesting	exaggeration
kettle	mineral	available	elementary
never	disgraceful	introduction	similarity
morning	telegraph	understanding	classification
careful	catalogue	appropriate	discriminative
second	companion	occupation	astrological
poem	dictation	activities	introductory
rhyming	history	invitation	equivalency
salad	holiday	equivalent	regulatory
children	important	community	
question	tournament	transportation	
learning	widening	Indonesian	
brother	Canada	composition	

Rhyming

The ability to recognize rhyme requires an underlying awareness that rhyming words end with the same group of sounds.

Children are given 'odd man out' tasks where they identify the word in a group that does not rhyme.

Thinking of and saying their own rhyming word in response to a given word is more difficult and is done a little later.

When words that rhyme are matched to their written equivalents, similarities in letter patterns can be observed. At the same time differences can be noted. This provides an opportunity for teachers to introduce spelling rules.

Rhyming — Same or Different?

• •

The teacher reads the word pairs while the children listen and indicate rhyming or non-rhyming pairs.

two–shoe	feet–beat	hand–band
red–bed	ten–when	blue–cat
fish–wish	round–play	cup–pup
hug–will	zoom–room	ship–lip
snap–cap	wait–rate	talk–shoe
hall–wall	pen–fat	thin–race
sun–fun	car–star	bed–wed
four–tree	cook–look	stone–bone

YES and **NO** cards (p. 86) can be used as alternatives for the same/different cards.

Cut out **YES** and **NO** cards and paste on thick card.

Suggested uses
- Each child has a **YES** and **NO** card and uses them to indicate if the two words spoken by the teacher rhyme.
- **YES** and **NO** cards are used to indicate if target vowel is in the word spoken by the teacher. See sound analysis section. **Cut and Sort** (p. 151).
- Activities on pages 84 and 85 are best suited for small groups of four to six students.

Three Word Rhyme

Read these words to the children. The children say if the three words rhyme or not. The **YES** and **NO** cards may also be used.

bear	chair	stare
car	far	bar
door	mat	big
bell	ring	cap
ball	hall	small
rug	tug	bug
head	red	bed
thing	hand	talk
show	grow	bow
bad	sad	mad
fish	boy	cat
walk	talk	hawk
sand	hand	band
free	see	bee
card	ship	big
wish	dish	fish
play	day	say
dog	log	fog

As an extension activity, ask the children to make up a sentence using all three rhyming words.

For example: The **dog** hid in the **log** during the **fog**.

YES ✓

NO ✗

same

different

A SOUND WAY: PHONICS ACTIVITIES FOR EARLY LITERACY © 1996. Permission is granted for the purchaser to photocopy this page for non-commercial classroom use. Pembroke Publishers.

Skill:	Recognizing rhyming and non-rhyming words.
Teacher's Notes:	Read lists of word pairs. Children hold up the **same** or **different**, or **yes** or **no** cards to indicate if words sound the same or different, or if they rhyme or not.
See also:	**Three Word Rhyme** (p. 85), **Cut and Sort** (p. 151), **Rhyming Snap** (pp. 88-90).

COLOUR/Rhyme 1

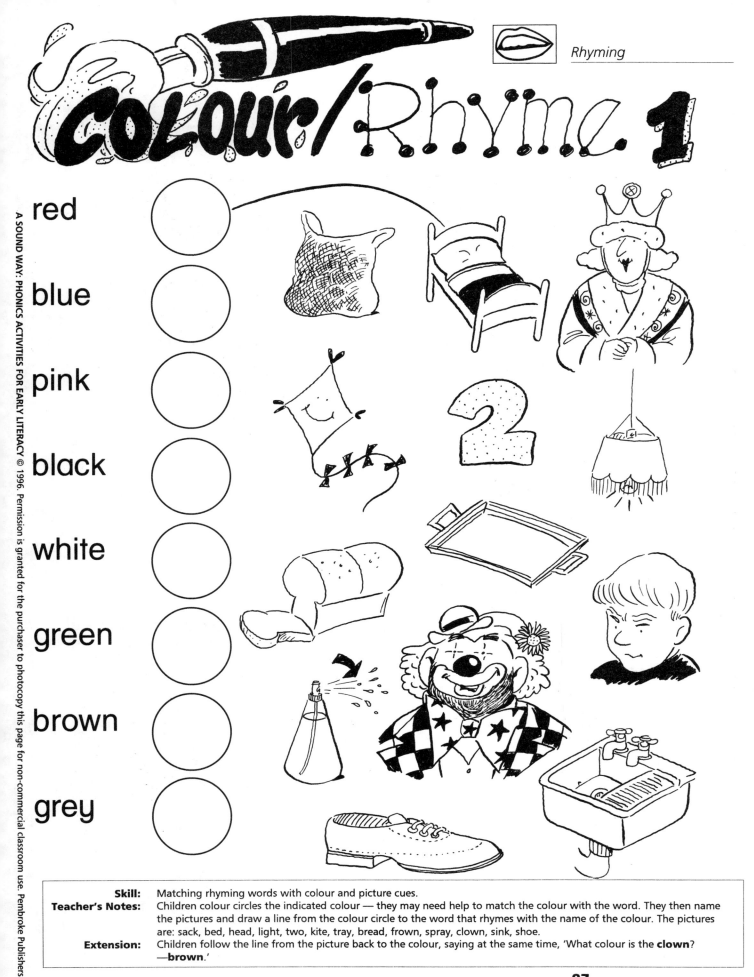

red

blue

pink

black

white

green

brown

grey

Skill:	Matching rhyming words with colour and picture cues.
Teacher's Notes:	Children colour circles the indicated colour — they may need help to match the colour with the word. They then name the pictures and draw a line from the colour circle to the word that rhymes with the name of the colour. The pictures are: sack, bed, head, light, two, kite, tray, bread, frown, spray, clown, sink, shoe.
Extension:	Children follow the line from the picture back to the colour, saying at the same time, 'What colour is the **clown**? —**brown**.'

Rhyming Snap

- Familiarize children with the names of all pictures on pages 89 and 90, then cut them into separate cards. In a simple version of the game the teacher holds all cards and places them in turn onto a pile that all the children can see. The children indicate a rhyming pair by calling out '**SNAP**'.

- The cards can be divided evenly between two players. Each player places a picture card in turn face up on a table or the floor. The child who identifies the rhyming pair by calling '**SNAP**' collects the cards. The winner is the player who has won all the cards from his/ her opponent.

Pictures used in Rhyming Snap

sail tail snail nail

sock rock clock block lock

tap cap snap map

key tree bee knee free

bell shell

chair bear pear hair

- For variety, (and a challenge) remove the pictures for **lock** and **free** and with the remaining pictures play Concentration. Turn all the cards face down. Take turns to turn up two cards. If they rhyme, keep them.

Rhyming Snap (i)

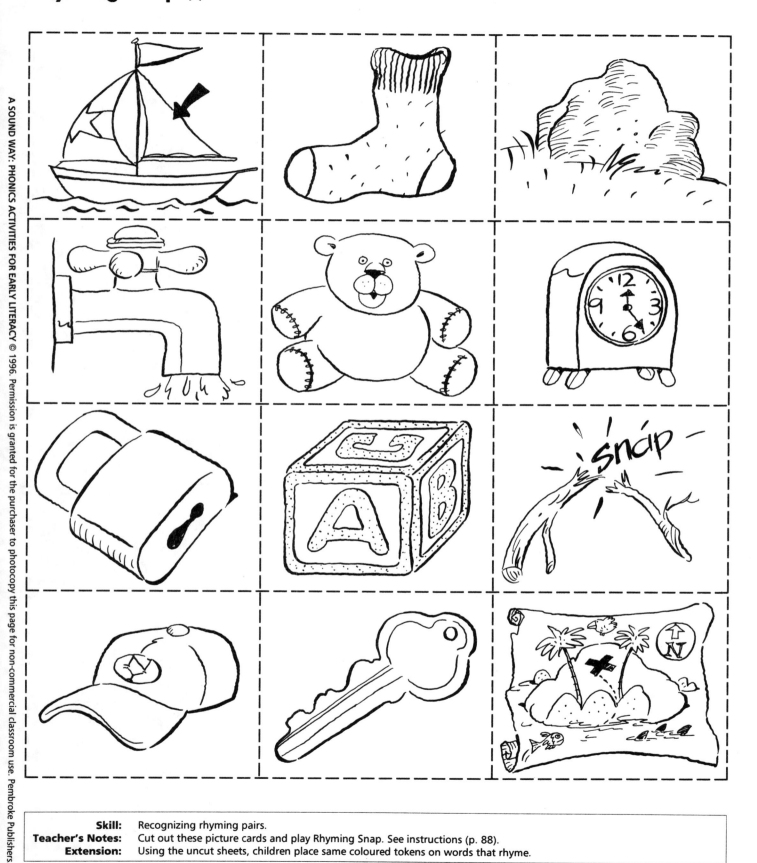

Skill:	Recognizing rhyming pairs.
Teacher's Notes:	Cut out these picture cards and play Rhyming Snap. See instructions (p. 88).
Extension:	Using the uncut sheets, children place same coloured tokens on words that rhyme.

Rhyming Snap (ii)

Skill:	Recognizing rhyming pairs.	
Teacher's Notes:	Cut out these picture cards and play Rhyming Snap. See instructions (p. 88).	
Extension:	Using the uncut sheets, children place same coloured tokens on words that rhyme.	

Skill:	Recognizing two rhyming words within a spoken sentence.
Teacher's Notes:	See instructions (p. 92). More matching shapes can be drawn by the children on the reverse side of this page.
See also:	**Rhyming Sentences** (p. 108).
Extension:	Choose one rhyming pair from p. 92 and write the words on the board. Do the children notice any similarities in the spelling of these words? For example, mouse-house, rat-cat.

Rhyming Sentences
(To accompany Draw a Rhyme 1 page 91)

Children draw the two rhyming words in matching shapes, i.e. two circles or two squares. Modify examples as necessary to target the skill level of your class, individual students and their drawing ability.

I tripped on a **rake**
and dropped the **cake**.

The wind blew my new **balloon**
up and up, to the **moon**.

We have a little **mouse**
living in our **house**.

I paid all my **money**
to buy this beautiful **bunny**.

Tabby is a clever **cat**.
One day she caught a grey **rat**.

Sally was only very **small**
but she still played with a yellow **ball**.

Dad saw a dirty **fly**
walking on Mum's apple **pie**.

I left my **coat**
in Dad's speed **boat**.

Ooey gooey **egg**
is running down my **leg**.

I stood on the **chair**
to cut my **hair**.

Have the children make up their own Draw a Rhyme to say to a friend.

Follow That Rhyme

Read the following rhymes. Children complete the actions and say which two words rhyme.

Tap your **head**, then find something **red**.

Wiggle your **hips,** and lick your **lips**.

Put your hand on your **knee,** and find a letter **T**.

Give your hands a **clap,** then lay them in your **lap**.

Walk to the **door** and sit on the **floor**.

Give your eye a **wink,** and have a big **think**.

Pretend you're a **tree,** then count to **three**.

Put your hand on the **table** and jump if you're **able**.

Count to **ten,** then find the teacher's **pen**.

Make a face like a **fish,** then make a **wish**.

Look for something **blue,** then point to your **shoe**.

Touch your **toe,** and then say **'No'**.

Make a sign for **stop,** then take a big **hop**.

Find a picture on the **wall,** now look around for something **small**.

Put your elbow on your **knee,** now tell me something you can **see**.

Pretend you're a **bear,** and stand on a **chair**.

Count to **seven,** then say the number **eleven**.

Point to a **friend,** because this is the **end**.

Extend the task further by giving the first stage of a direction and have children supply the end rhyming word.
For example: Have a **wish**, then catch a . . .
         Stand up **straight** and say number . . .

RHYMING PAIRS 1 PEARS

Skill: Matching rhyming pictures.
Teacher's Notes: Children say the name of each picture and find the pairs of words that rhyme. The rhyming pairs on this page are: pen-ten, fish-dish, sun-run, dog-log, net-wet, hat-cat, hug-mug. This activity is not for beginning readers. It is more appropriate for students who are familiar with or ready for an introduction to word families.
See also: **Rhyming Pairs 2** (p. 95).
Extension: Children choose one pair of rhyming words and make a sentence using both of them. Let them draw the sentence.

RHYMING PAIRS 2 ~~PEARS~~

Rhyming

Skill:	Matching rhyming pictures.
Teacher's Notes:	Children say the name of each picture and find the pairs of words that rhyme. The rhyming pairs on this page are: tree-three, feet-seat, bone-phone, coat-boat, tail-snail, spoon-moon, rake-cake, kite-light.
See also:	**Rhyming Pairs 1** (p. 94).
Extension:	Children choose one pair of rhyming words and make a sentence using both of them. Let them draw the sentence.

A Rhyme in Time

All the animals have gathered together! Ask children to complete each line with a rhyming word to get the full picture.
For example: There was a **pig** who danced a **jig.**

Note: If children find this too difficult, give the first sound as a clue.

There was a **cat** who grew so _____ .

There was a **snail** who read my _____ .

There was a **dog** who jumped over a _____ .

There was a **mouse** who came from my _____ .

There was a **parrot** who always ate _____ .

There was a **snake** who much preferred _____ .

There was a **worm** who felt very _____ .

There was a **bear** whose hair was _____ .

There was an **alligator** who said she'd come _____ .

There was a **giraffe** who made me _____ .

There was a **fox** asleep in a _____ .

There was a **shark** who tried to _____ .

There was a **sheep** who arrived in a _____ .

There was a **fish** who made a _____ .

There was a **goat** who rowed the _____ .

There was a **deer** who only drank _____ .

Suggested answers: fat, mail, log, house, carrot, cake, firm, fair, later, laugh, box, bark, jeep, wish, boat, beer.

The RHYMERS

Rhyming

Skill: Rhyming words with nonsense names.
Teacher's Notes: See instructions (p. 98).

The Rhymers

Use the figures on page 97 (or get the children to create their own wonderful figures) to stimulate the children to think of rhyming words.

Provide a theme (see list of suggestions below) and a name for each figure in turn — choosing names that rhyme with well-known words belonging to the theme. For example:

Theme — shopping at the supermarket

Stacey **Stoghurt** bought some . . . . . (**yoghurt**)

Barry **Bilk** bought the . . . . . (**milk**)

- Fruit and vegetable shop
  Katy Keys bought some **peas**.

- Body parts
  Mrs Peck hurt her **neck**.

- Colours
  Gary Goo likes to wear **blue**.

- Clothes (a windy day caused some loss from the clothes line!)
  Mrs Hocking lost her **stocking**.

- Sports
  Robbie Rolf loves to play **golf**.

- Feelings
  Helen Hoss feels very **cross**.

After giving the theme and supplying the stimulus name, if the child still has difficulty supplying the rhyming word, simplify the task by giving additional clues at a meaning level. For example **peas** — 'they're green and round, and can also be bought frozen and in a packet'. The initial sound '**p**' can be given as another clue.

For variation and extension reverse the task. Select a word from a theme, for example: hockey (sport). The children choose a character and give it a name that rhymes such as **Mr Lockey** plays **hockey**.

My RHYMING PICTURES

For example

Skill:	Drawing a picture to complete a rhyming picture pair.
Teacher's Notes:	Children look at the picture and say its name and then think of a word that rhymes with it. Have them say the word then draw a picture of it.
See also:	**Rhyming Snap** (p. 88).
Extension:	Children cut up the completed sheet and play **Rhyming Snap** or **Concentration**.

Odd Man Out

Skill: Recognizing a word that does not belong in a given category.
Teacher's Notes: Cut out the Odd Man Out Card and paste it on to heavy card. Children could colour it in. See p. 101 for activities.

A SOUND WAY: PHONICS ACTIVITIES FOR EARLY LITERACY © 1996. Permission is granted for the purchaser to photocopy this page for non-commercial classroom use. Pembroke Publishers.

Odd Man Out

The **Odd Man Out card** can be used in a number of activities:
- rhyme activity 1 (below),
- first sound isolation, consonant (pp. 123-137) and vowel,
- last sound isolation (use words chosen from **Regular Words**, p. 149,
- medial vowel isolation (use words chosen from **Regular Words**, p. 149).

The card is held up by the child to signal the word which does not fit in to the group. The card can also be used in group activities. When children hear a word that doesn't fit in, they place their hand on the card.

Activity 1

'I'm going to tell you a word family. All the members of this family rhyme. Listen carefully and hold up your **Odd Man Out card** when you hear a word that doesn't belong in the word family.'
Here are some examples.
- This is the **ug** family:
  bug rug tug [**fan***] mug hug thug [**wet***] jug pug shrug.
- This is the **all** family:
  wall small hall call [**big***] ball tall [**run**] mall fall Paul [**went***]

Continue with other families. Try:

ed, ust, an, alk, og, ell, and, ar, ig, ue, est, en, ang, ing, end.

Activity 2

You can make the **Odd Man Out** task more difficult by increasing the similarity between the rhyming family and the **Odd Man Out**. See word families above. Replace asterisked words with the following alternatives.
For example: **ug** family — ***wig *jog**.
These words differ from the **ug** family by one sound only.
Other examples: **all** family — ***bought *wart**
                    ing family — ***dong *think**
                    end family — ***hand *Ben**

Now try these with your students.

This is the **ock** family: lock rock shock [**jog**] block clock mock [**back**] frock.
This is the **est** family: west rest [**post**] pest nest crest best test [**mess**].

Challenge the children! Can the Odd Man Out word be changed to fit in? For example: **bug, rug, tug, fan** — becomes **fug**.
Is it now a real or a nonsense word?

Read the word in the box.

Think of a word that rhymes with it.

Say the word—then draw a picture of it in the space.

date	pool	boys	loud
cork	boot	mouse	tart
burn	cone	boil	pain
beach	beef	lime	hook

Skill: Drawing a picture that rhymes with a written word.
Extension: Children write the word for each picture and then underline the letters that the two rhyming words have in common.

102

A SOUND WAY: PHONICS ACTIVITIES FOR EARLY LITERACY © 1996. Permission is granted for the purchaser to photocopy this page for non-commercial classroom use. Pembroke Publishers.

Underline the **rhyming** words and draw a picture showing these words. The first has been done for you.

My old tabby <u>cat</u>
Has caught a grey <u>rat</u>.

An angry king
Always wears a purple ring.

Tommy did a handstand
Looking at a rock band.

Sam is nearly fast asleep.
He left his clothes in a heap.

Mum is in the caravan
Cooking sausages in a pan.

A SOUND WAY: PHONICS ACTIVITIES FOR EARLY LITERACY © 1996. Permission is granted for the purchaser to photocopy this page for non-commercial classroom use. Pembroke Publishers.

Skill: Recognizing rhyming words in written text. Drawing a picture to show an understanding of the two-lined rhyme.
Teacher's Notes: This is a good reading exercise for introducing children to poetic form.
Extension: Children make up one rhyme of their own and give it to a friend to share.

COLOUR RHYME 2

Colour the circles in the colours indicated.

Read the words in the paint pallet.

Find all words that rhyme with the name of the colours in the circles. Colour them the right colours.

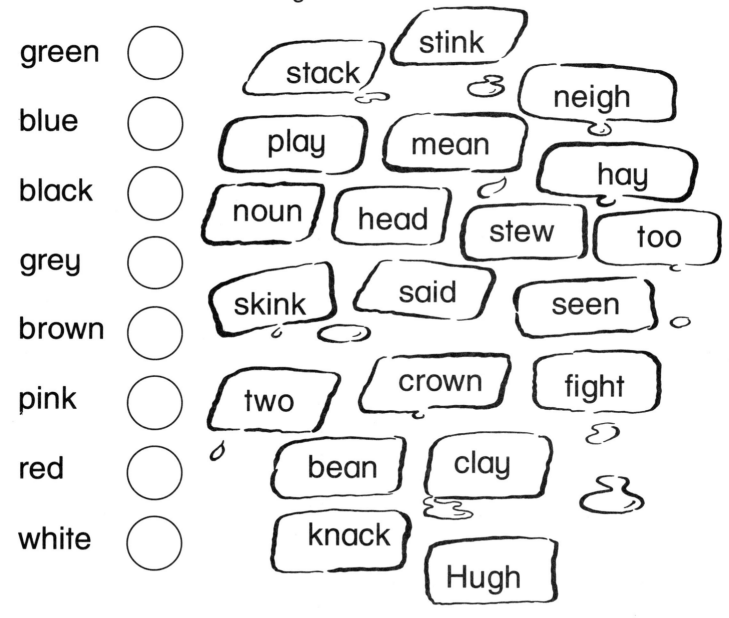

green ◯

blue ◯

black ◯

grey ◯

brown ◯

pink ◯

red ◯

white ◯

stink

stack

neigh

play   mean

hay

noun   head   stew   too

skink   said   seen

crown   fight

two

bean   clay

knack

Hugh

A SOUND WAY: PHONICS ACTIVITIES FOR EARLY LITERACY © 1996. Permission is granted for the purchaser to photocopy this page for non-commercial classroom use. Pembroke Publishers.

Skill:	Matching colour names with written rhyming words.
Teacher's Notes:	Earlier activities have built an awareness of rhymes. This activity asks children to identify words that end with the same group of sounds, which helps teach spelling patterns. See activities on pages 105 and 106 also.
Extension:	Children choose one colour word and write a rhyming chain. Which colour has the longest chain?

Go up the ladders adding words to make rhyming pairs. Read the words out loud to make sure the pairs rhyme.

pen

rat

fill

log

hut

For example:

leg   peg

stop
flag
clock
skin
prank
trip
slot
spin
gram

it
up
in
at
egg
on

hand
went
nest
jump
hold
bank

Skill: Writing a word to complete rhyming pairs.
Extension: Children rewrite all their own words on a separate piece of paper and cut them out individually. They give them to a friend to sort onto his/her own ladders to make rhyming pairs.

Rhyming

Fill up the bubbles with words that rhyme.

Remember — rhyming words sound alike but may not look alike at all. The first bubble has been started for you.

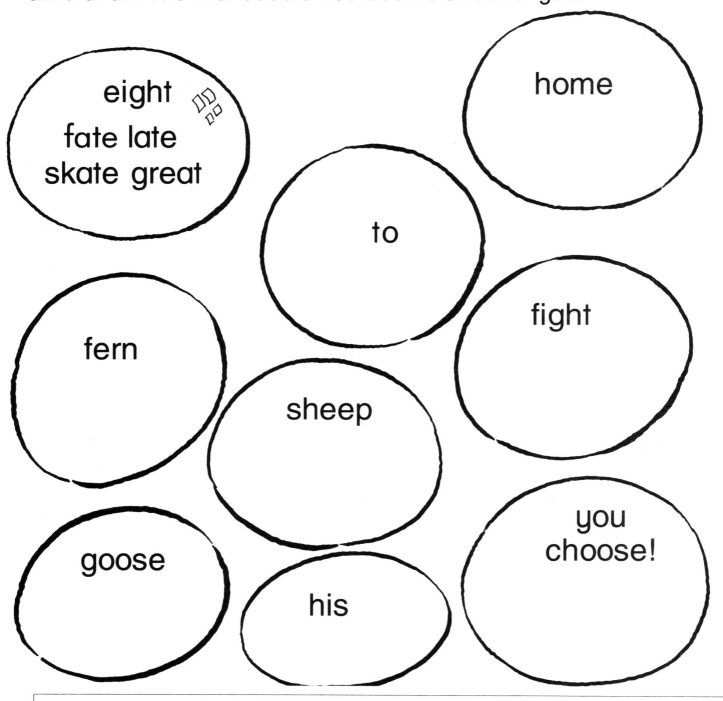

eight
fate late
skate great

home

to

fern

fight

sheep

goose

his

you
choose!

Skill: Writing rhyming words.
Extension: Children write groups of rhyming words on balloons and suspend them from the ceiling.

Re-rhyme Humpty Dumpty

The first line of *Humpty Dumpty* has changed. Read it, then make up a rhyming second line. <u>Underline</u> the rhyming words.

For example: Humpty Dumpty sat on a <u>bike</u>,

And bumped into his friend called <u>Mike</u>

1 Humpty Dumpty sat on a stool,

_____

2 Humpty Dumpty sat on a bed,

_____

3 Humpty Dumpty sat on a chair,

_____

4 Humpty Dumpty ate some pie,

_____

5 Humpty Dumpty ate some fruit,

_____

6 Humpty Dumpty ate some meat,

_____

7 Humpty Dumpty went to play,

_____

Skill: Completing a rhyming couplet.
Extension: Children rerhyme another nursery rhyme, for example, Incy Wincy Spider. **Or**, give each pair of students the first line of a rhyme. Together, they complete the second line and share it with the class.

Can you write a poem by completing the two lines below? The last words must rhyme.

For example: I'd rather be a little **fox**

Than have to wear my Father's **sox**

1 There once was a ....

    Who ....

2 Would you wear a ....

    If ....

3 Should you go to ....

    When ....

4 Can you build a ....

    And ....

5 I'd rather be a ....

    Than ....

Skill: Completing both lines of a rhyming couplet.
See also: Resource list for rhyme (p. 220).
Extension: Read limericks from _Edward Lear_ and then, as a class, make up your own.

Do They Rhyme?

The mirrors below contain words that look similar.
Cross out the word that does **not** rhyme with the others.

Rhyming

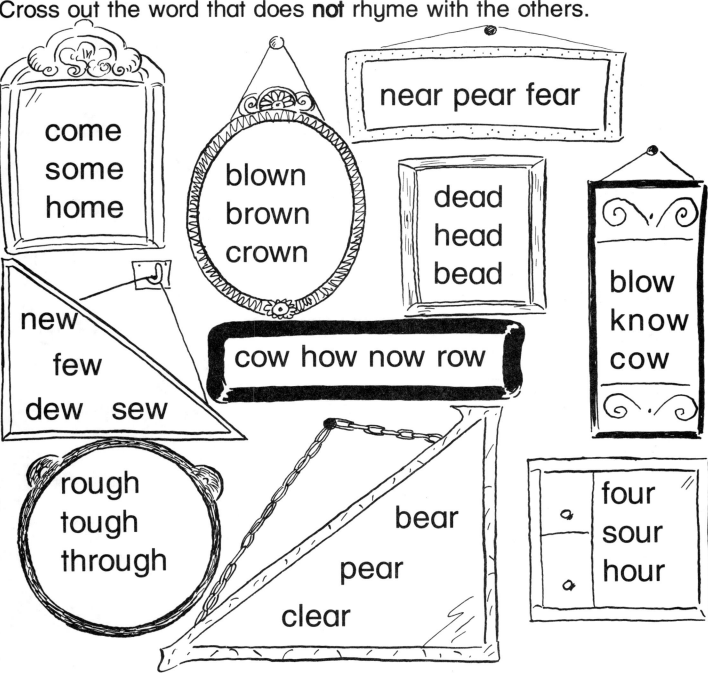

come
some
home

near pear fear

blown
brown
crown

dead
head
bead

blow
know
cow

new
few
dew   sew

cow how now row

rough
tough
through

bear
pear
clear

four
sour
hour

Skill: Detecting rhyming words from words which look alike.
Extension: Children select the word in each group that does not rhyme and write down three words that rhyme with this word. Do
                these look alike or different? For example, dead, head, **bead** — lead, feed, read.

A SOUND WAY: PHONICS ACTIVITIES FOR EARLY LITERACY © 1996. Permission is granted for the purchaser to photocopy this page for non-commercial classroom use. Pembroke Publishers.

109

Rhyming Challenge

Read the words. Join words that rhyme using a different colour pencil for each group of words.

Remember — rhyming words do not have to look alike.
— some words which look the same do not rhyme.

e.g.

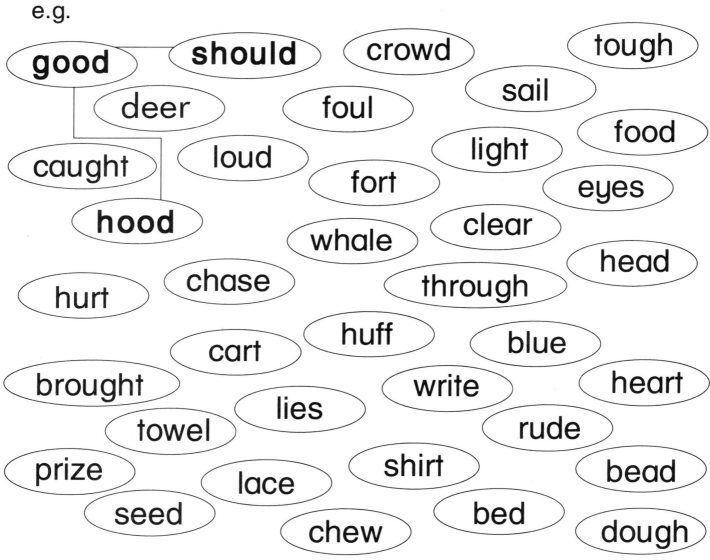

Skill:	Recognizing rhyming words from visually confusing words.
Extension:	Children choose the names of five fruits or vegetables and then think of three words that rhyme with each of them. They write them down and circle those which are spelt in a similar way.

Alliteration

Alliteration involves the beginning-sound analysis skill — being aware of the first sound in words.

Children are required to recognize and later provide words that begin with the same sound.

When written words are involved, children will come to understand that the letter equivalents of a sound are not always the same.

Sound Stories 1

This activity can be done orally or as a written task for more advanced students.

Children fill in each blank space with a word that starts with the **'sss'** sound.

_____ went on a trip to _____ .

He went with his friend _____ .

They packed _____ and a _____ .

They travelled by _____ .

And on the way they played _____ and ate _____ .

Repeat the task using in turn — **'f', 'g', 'd', 'm', 'l'**

Then ask children to complete the task using the first sound of their own name.

Sneaky Sounds

Read the following sentences. Children discover the alliteration. Further classroom suggestions are on page 113.

Billy **B**igilo **b**uilt **b**ig **b**oats.
Sammy **S**mith **s**aw **s**ix **c**entipedes.
Karen **K**ephard **k**eeps **c**ute **k**ittens.
Leslie **L**ittle **l**ikes **l**emon **l**ollipops.
Sharon **S**chiller **s**hares **s**ugar **s**herberts.
Denis **D**avidson **d**oes **d**ifficult **d**ecimals.
Fiona **F**etter **p**hotographs **f**urry **f**oxes.
Nellie **K**nowles **k**nows **N**eville **N**estles.
Robert **R**ollins **w**rites **r**idiculous **r**hymes.
Penny **P**orter **p**aints **p**erfect **p**ansies.
George **J**effries **j**uggled **g**iant **j**ellybeans.

As an extension activity write one or more of the sentences on the board and encourage children to observe the different spelling patterns which achieve the sound alliteration.

'I Went Shopping and I Bought . . .'

• •

Play it Orally

Choose a sound such as **'mm'**.

One child starts — 'I went shopping and I bought **m**eat.'

Next child — either merely thinks of another word or recalls previous one and adds to it. 'I went shopping and I bought **m**eat and a **m**op.'

You may wish to show the letter for the sound, e.g. ⌐c⌐ but you will have to specify the sound, e.g. **'c'** as in **c**orn to avoid confusion.

Play it Visually

Place cards showing selected letters and digraphs face down.

Children take turns to turn a card and the game is played as above with the letter shown on the card.

Children will be focusing on the letter so their list of words may begin with different sounds. For example: **'ch'** — *ch*ewing gum, *ch*rome

Play with dice. Each child thinks of the number of words on the die.

Keep your language about letters and sounds clear!

Further Suggestions for Classroom Alliteration

• Play 'I went shopping'. Vary the game by substituting 'I went to a barbecue and I took . . .' or 'On the weekend I . . .'

• Select children randomly and ask them to think of a verb that starts with the same sound as their names.
  For example: Sam smiles. Karen claps.

• Use the many books that stress alliteration as a basis for learning about sounds. See **Resource List** (p. 220). Children then make their own books. This is a good introduction to the remaining activities in this section.

• Use alliteration in conjunction with the **Sound Bucket Game** (p. 123). The child takes out an object and thinks of an associated word beginning with the same sound. For example: The child takes a ball out of the bucket and says, 'bouncing ball'.

Sound Stories

Write an alliterative story about one of the following characters.
Start as many words as you can with the same sound.

For example: **Penny Pollard**. Make a word bank first.
Use the back of this page.

> paddock pumpkin pulled people poodle picnic
> potatoes parcel pranced put popcorn private

Penny Pollard packed popcorn and potatoes.
Penny's picnic . . .

Fearful Freddy
Heroic Helen
Prince the Pony
Shy Sharon
Albert the Alligator
Stinky Steven
Dangerous David
Lucky Lucy
Michael the Magician

Skill: Producing alliterative sentences.
Extension: As a class, children create an alliterative story such as 'the party'. The sound for alliteration changes with each sentence. The teacher can indicate the sound by holding up the letter or saying the sound. For example, Betty and Bruce broke Benny's ball, Cathy cried 'cause Colin couldn't cut the cake.

Give these teams alliterative names. Colour their team shirts.

Moncton
Monsters

Toronto
_____

_____
Dragons

Calgary
_____

_____
Sharks

Victoria
_____

Skill: Producing two-word alliteration.
Extension: Children think up four of their own teams that have alliterative names.

Jobs

Give these people jobs that start with the same sound as their first names.

For example: Fred Frost the **farmer**.

Peter Patterson the _____

Sally Scot the _____

Denis Daley the _____

Robert Rogers the _____

Terry Thomas the _____

Linda Luff the _____

NOW make up two of your own.

_____

_____

Skill: Using alliteration.
Extension: In a small group, children create a play using alliterative characters.

A SOUND WAY: PHONICS ACTIVITIES FOR EARLY LITERACY © 1996. Permission is granted for the purchaser to photocopy this page for non-commercial classroom use. Pembroke Publishers.

BAD HABITS

Discover what **bad habits** these people have. Match a face with a sentence. Write in their names — make sure the names start with the same sound as the bad habit.

Neville _____ _____ _____ _____

Neville never notices Nelly's nice netball.

_____ seldom smiles sweetly.

_____ blows big bubbles with his blueberry bubblegum.

_____ draws dead dogs and dreadful dragons.

_____ carelessly kicks cute kittens.

Skill: Using alliteration.
Extension: Children discuss bad habits people have in the community, for example, nibbling nails, driving dangerously, picking pimples.

117

GOODHABITS

Make up **good habits** for these characters.

For example: Mandy makes marvellous music.

Lucy   Tommy   James   David

Write good habit tongue-twisters for these children, using the same first sounds in each word.

Lucy _____

_____

Tommy _____

_____

James _____

_____

David _____

_____

Skill:	Writing alliterative sentences.
Teacher's Notes:	If you wish to work on particular consonant blends, this activity can be adapted using names with consonant blends, for example, Steven, Brian, Fred, Stephanie.
Extension:	Each child draws a person and writes an alliterative sentence. These are combined to make a class reader.

Alliterative Sentences

Create your own alliterative sentences.

p Peter Piper played ping pong.

s _____

l _____

m _____

r _____

f _____

t _____

d _____

n _____

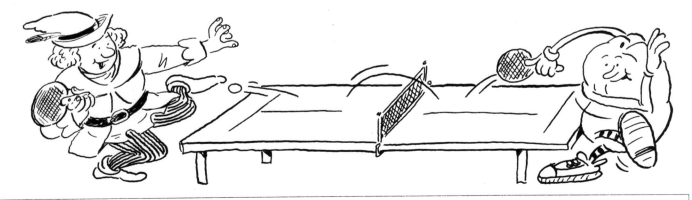

Skill: Writing alliterative sentences.
Extension: Children pretend that Fearless Freddy or Careless Cathy came to their house to play. What would they say? (Remember they must speak in alliteration.)

Analysis

Activities in this section provide children with experience in breaking words into their component sounds.

Some focus is placed on initial and final sounds and special emphasis is given to vowels, both long and short.

There are specific activities for blends because children often find it difficult to 'find' the sounds in blends.

The use of concrete materials to represent the sounds (e.g. buttons, counters, boxes drawn on paper) will give the children guidance in listening for the sounds and later in choosing the corresponding letters for these sounds.

These activities have a practical application for spelling. For example, see activities which deal with vowels on pages 151, 153–155 and 157.

Listening Corner

• •

- Programming a regular time for listening activities is important.
- If possible, work with a small group of children rather than the whole class.
- Prepare a comfortable area, perhaps in a corner, using cushions to sit on etc.
- For younger children you can symbolize that it is a quiet listening time by introducing a puppet. For example: a rabbit puppet with large ears. Cardboard ears attached to a headband also work well.
- Activities that highlight rhyme, sound analysis, blending, and manipulation skills can be used in the listening corner. For example:
  - 'Clap your hands if your name rhymes with **peel**.' (Neil)
  - 'How many girls' names do you know starting with the **'l'** sound?'
  - go around the circle. Lucy, Lena . . .
  - 'Help me finish this sentence —
    I've been on holidays in **B** . . . . .
    I fell over and hurt my **l** . . . .'
  - Find the word — **'c'–'r'–'a'–'ck'.**
- There will be opportunities for incidental activities during classroom routines. For example:
  - 'Would this person please take a note to the Principal — **'m'–'ar'–'g'–'ie''**
  - Line up all children whose name begins with **'s'** sound.
- Record some activities onto tape and use these in conjunction with activities in this book such as **Rolly the Rabbit** (p. 158). A small group of children can do the activity at a **Listening Post**, using headphones.

Sound Bucket Game

Place everyday objects in a bucket or bag. Choose objects suitable for your class learning outcome. For example:

- isolating initial sounds
  's', 'f', 'm', 'b', 'l', 't', 'a'
  apple **s**ock, **m**ouse, **t**ile, **l**ollipop, **b**all, **f**an.

- isolating initial consonant blends
  frog **cl**ock **st**amp **bl**ock

Children take turns to choose an object. They:
- say the name of it,
- find what sound it begins with, then
- think of another word which begins with the same sound.

Variation

Throw dice.
    Think of this number of words, all of which begin with the same sound as the item selected from the bucket.
    Go around the circle, each child thinking of a word beginning with the target sound until the required number is reached.
Rhyme can also be the aim of this game.

Extension

Using a chart of letters of the alphabet, place objects onto the appropriate beginning letter.

Copy Cat

Some children have difficulty isolating the sounds within words. This activity builds awareness of sounds and helps identify and isolate sounds within words. **Copy Cat** game can be used to introduce gentle progressions.

The class or child is asked to imitate sounds made by the teacher or puppet.

1   The teacher says **'mm'**, **'nn'**, **'sss'**, **'p'**, **'k'**, **'rrr'**, **'fff'** etc. The children **copy** each sound as they hear it. This activity follows on naturally from activities such as **Mr Mouth** (p. 16) and **Mr Tongue's House** (p. 17).

2   The teacher says a series of words which begin with the same sound. They can also intersperse the sound if required.
For example: munch, mouth, (**'mmm'**) monkey, monster, marmalade, (**'mmm'**) . . . etc.
The children **copy cat** the teacher's words and sounds.

3   When children are confident with step 2, they can contribute either a new word beginning with the sound or supply the sound at the end of the series of words said by the teacher.

4   The teacher makes the sound and the children copy but also say a word that starts with that sound. For example:
Teacher — **'ff'**, children — **'ff'**–fish

5   Children can take the role of the teacher or play with a partner.

Extension: Repeat the activity with the focus on the final sound of words. For example:
fat, eight, note, (**'ttt'**),
fight, heart, robot.

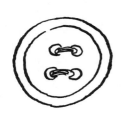

Skill:	Matching pictures that begin with the same sound.
Teacher's Notes:	In this activity children listen for and isolate the initial word sounds for each picture then match the pictures that begin with the same sound by colouring them the same colour, drawing a line etc.
Extension:	Children decorate a sheet of paper with cut out pictures that start with the same sound as their own name.

125

Analysis

First **sound** snap

Skill:	Recognizing words that begin with the same sound.	
Teacher's Notes:	Cut out the pictures and paste onto card. The game may be played with the teacher presenting the cards. Show the picture and ask children to say 'SNAP' if the first consonants match.	
	Words on this page: bone, fire, tie, balloon, boat, football, bag, fruit, nail, nose, fish, ten.	
See also:	**First Sound Snap** (pp. 127-129) and **First Sound Dominoes** (pp. 130-132).	
Extension:	Children sort the pictures into the correct **sound boxes** (each sound box has a letter and/or a picture to represent the sound, for example, '**b**' bus).	

First Sound Snap (2)

Skill: Recognizing words that begin with the same sound.
Teacher's Notes: Words on this page: leaf, leg, rod, lock, lips, wink, web, rain, road, wine, worm, rabbit.
See also: **First Sound Snap** (pp. 126, 128, 129) and **First Sound Dominoes** (pp. 130-132).

127

First Sound Snap (3)

Skill:	Recognizing words that begin with the same sound.
Teacher's Notes:	Words on this page: nest, tent, cup, car, needle, toe, core, card, hard, hammer, heart, house.
See also:	**First Sound Snap** (pp. 126, 127, 129) and **First Sound Dominoes** (pp. 130-132).
Alternative:	Divide the pack between two children. They take turns to play a card, saying 'SNAP' and collecting the cards if the first consonants match.

First Sound Snap (4)

Skill:	Recognizing words that begin with the same sound.	
Teacher's Notes:	Words on this page: puppet, six, milk, pan, pin, sock, sun, mitten, pie, mop, moon, seal. In all the **First Sound Snap** exercises, there are four words for each sound: **'b', 'f', 't', 'n', 'c', 'h', 'l', 'w', 'r', 'p', 's', 'm'**. Introduce easily confused sounds separately. For example, **'r'/'w'/, 'p'/'b', 'm'/'n'**.	
See also:	**First Sound Snap** (pp. 126-128) and **First Sound Dominoes** (pp. 130-132).	

First Sound Dominoes

Analysis

Skill: Matching words that begin with the same sound.
Teacher's Notes: Instructions (p. 133).
See also: **First Sound Dominoes** (pp. 131-132) and **First Sound Snap** (pp. 126-129).

130

A SOUND WAY: PHONICS ACTIVITIES FOR EARLY LITERACY © 1996. Permission is granted for the purchaser to photocopy this page for non-commercial classroom use. Pembroke Publishers.

First Sound Dominoes

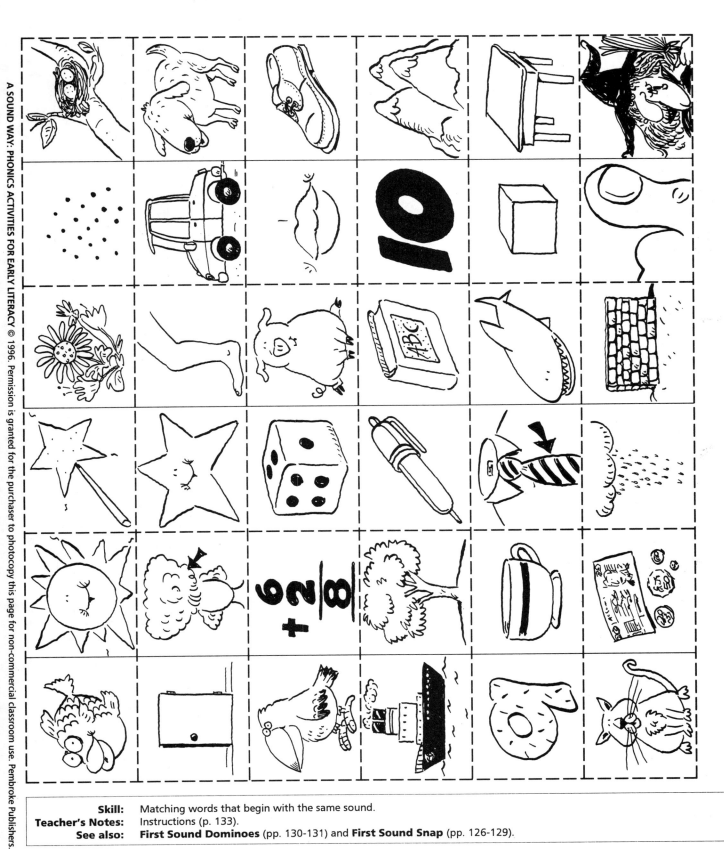

Skill:	Matching words that begin with the same sound.
Teacher's Notes:	Instructions (p. 133).
See also:	**First Sound Dominoes** (pp. 130-131) and **First Sound Snap** (pp. 126-129).

Make Your Own
First Sound Dominoes

Skill:	Matching words that begin with the same sound.
Teacher's Notes:	Instructions (p. 133).
See also:	**First Sound Dominoes** (pp. 131-133) and **First Sound Snap** (pp. 126-129).

First Sound Dominoes

1 (p. 130)

mat–teeth,	net–cake
shapes–four,	ring–ball
man–light,	duck–rat
three–pin,	leaf–flag
window–can,	map–bed
snake–bone,	shirt–pan
bat–letter,	card–mitten
thong–fence,	pear–web
sock–rabbit,	nail–balloons

2 (p. 131)

fish–sun,	wand–flowers
dots–nest,	door–wig
star–leg,	car–dog
bird–sum,	dice–pig
mouth–shoe,	ship–tree
pen–book,	ten–mountains
nine–cup,	tie–shark
box–table,	cat–money
rain–wall,	thumb–witch

Instructions

Make cards by cutting along the dashed lines on pages 130 and 131.

Distribute the cards evenly among three or more players.

The person with the **net/cake** card begins by placing it face up. In turn, players add a card to either end of the line by joining pictures that begin with the same sound.

Play ends when no more pictures can be matched up. The person with the least cards left over is the winner.

First Sound Dominoes — Extension

1   Use the blank domino cards (see p. 132) to make further **First Sound Dominoes**.

2   Use these cards to write words for a picture–word **Dominoes** game.

3   Use the blank domino cards to write single letters for a picture–letter match activity.

4   Use the blank domino cards to write the first letter for each picture and glue these to the reverse of the picture dominoes so that players can check their responses as they play.

Odd First Sound Out

• •

Instructions

• The teacher shows the children the picture page headed **Odd First Sound Out** (pp. 135–137).
• The teacher points to the first group of three pictures and names each picture.
• The teacher then says 'Hold up your Odd Man Out Card (p. 100) when I say the word that **does not** start with the same sound as the other words. Listen again, Car — balloon — bed. **Car** is the Odd Man Out because it **does not** start with **'b'**.' (Word groups may need to be repeated several times.)

1 (p. 135)

(car)	balloon	bed
(girl)	log	leg
rabbit	ribbon	(map)
(tree)	finger	football

2 (p. 136)

saw	(phone)	sing
cake	king	(pencil)
parcel	pin	(van)
milk	(teddy)	mountain

3 (p. 137)

(bag)	sun	seat
dinosaur	(pencil)	dog
fish	fork	(cup)
(book)	key	kite

Odd First Sound Out (1)

Skill:	Discriminating first sounds in words.
Teacher's Notes:	Instructions (p. 134).

Odd First Sound Out (2)

Skill:	Discriminating first sounds in words.	
Teacher's Notes:	Instructions (p. 134).	

Odd First Sound Out (3)

Skill:	Discriminating first sounds in words.	
Teacher's Notes:	Instructions (p. 134).	

Thinking With Language

The aim of this task is for the children to complete sentences read aloud by the teacher. The children supply the missing word, using the context of the sentence and the initial sound as clues.

1 Last night we looked at the s _____.

2 The circus has a funny c _____.

3 Thunder makes a loud n _____.

4 Rosa knows how to cook t _____.

5 Don't jump on the b _____. It might b _____.

6 I love to eat s _____. It is my favourite f _____.

7 Let's go fly our k _____. I bet mine will go very h _____.

8 My brother is s _____ with the chicken pox.

9 Tom b _____ his arm while playing football.

10 A surfer rides a w _____ into shore.

11 The earthquake sh _____ the building.

12 The fish ate the w _____ on the hook.

13 The scouts set up their t _____ near the lake.

Extension

Lead the class to make up a story, e.g. about the holidays, a trip to the zoo, a scary night. At the end of each sentence the last word is omitted but the beginning sound clue is provided. The letter representing this sound is also shown.

Tails

· ·

Listen to these pairs of words. Do they end in the same sound?
Indicate your answer with the **YES** or **NO** card (p. 86).

Choose words from the list below that end in contrasting sounds, for
example: **'f' and 'g'** — **sniff** — **bag**.
   As the children become more confident select words that end in
sounds that are similar and therefore more easily confused by the
child.

For example: ha**d**–ha**t**, bu**s**–buz**z**, li**fe**–ha**ve**

The word lists with similar endings are grouped together for you.

s	**z**	**sh**	**ch**	**j**
bus	buzz	bush	beach	page
force	rose	fresh	torch	barge
mess	goes	mush	much	cage
race	raise	leash	search	rage
house	nose	crash	which	large

f	**v**	**th**	**t**	**d**
sniff	live	bath	pet	bored
laugh	save	north	write	ride
half	have	south	feet	feed
if	hive	myth	Kate	lied
cough	starve	both	snort	made

m	**n**	**ng**	**p**	**b**
home	line	sting	hope	cub
room	mean	rang	rope	robe
lime	main	sung	loop	tub
boom	corn	bring	help	bib
some	tune	thing	ship	rob

k	**g**	**l**
pick	pig	bell
back	bag	hole
lock	log	doll
cork	snug	pill
rake	beg	sail

What's in the Last Carriage?

Skill:	Identifying final sounds in words.
Teacher's Notes:	Explain that when we say words some sounds are at the beginning, some in the middle and others are at the end — just like this train. Have children roll dice and move tokens along the track. When they land, they say, feel and hear the last sound in each word, for example, girl — 'l'.
Extension:	Children say another word that **ends** with the same sound.

Sorting Sounds and Letters

Word sorting activities require sound analysis. Students need to think about individual sounds in words and sort them according to certain criteria.

* There are many picture and letter card resources in this book which can be used to facilitate sound awareness.
* Children can also sort pictures from magazines or small objects from the teacher's **sound bag** and match these to letters.
* Children can work independently or in pairs to sort pictures according to

    – number of sounds
    – final consonant
    – short or long vowel

    – initial consonant
    – medial vowel
    – consonant blend

Alternatives

* Children 'fish' for a picture from a **sound pond.**
* Children can create their own **Odd Man Out** sequence (see pp. 134–137).
* Children can set up **sound shops**, e.g. **'p'** or **'s'** shop.
* Children attach pictures with Velcro to class letter and alphabet charts or to game boards or felt board.
* Children post cards in the appropriate sound postbox, e.g. **'man'** in the **'m'** box.

Keep It Concrete

· ·

When finding **words** in sentences, **syllables** in words or **sounds** in words, children will find it easier if these can be represented in a concrete way.

Each child can be given a small container of
- buttons
- breadtags
- coloured counters
- small blocks (Lego)

These items can be used alone or in conjunction with the **grids** (see page 148) to represent the words, syllables or sounds. See **Feel and Find** (page 144).

Examples:

Spin — this word has four sounds. Can you find them in your mouth? As you find them put a counter in each square of the grid.

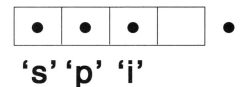

's' 'p' 'i'

Small blocks can be used in a similar way. They are fun for children to separate and push together (blending) as they explore sound awareness tasks.

For example:

fish

Fish has three sounds so put three blocks together. Say 'fish' — now say it slowly and find the three sounds in your mouth. As you find them move the blocks apart.

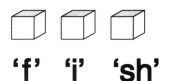

'f' 'i' 'sh'

Keep It Concrete

When letters are used children will enjoy and benefit from being able to handle and manipulate words in a similar way to the blocks, buttons etc. (See **Find the Sounds, then the Letters** p. 165.)

As children acquire reliable sound–letter links they can build up their own individual set of letters. For example:

 — firm cardboard

 — laminate sample squares or 'tiles' cut from Bristol board

— peg with label stuck on lower section

Note:

1 Different colours can be used for short vowels, long vowels and consonants.

2 Where a sound is represented by more than one letter it is still written on a card of the *same* size. For example: | ee | e |

3 **'ch', 'ph', 'th', 'wh', 'sh'** — should be the same colour as the other consonants

4 **'ll' 'ck' 'ss'** — the 2 letters are on one square because they represent *one* sound

Feel and Find the Sounds

• •

Use **Grids** (see p. 148) with buttons or counters, and choose words from either **Regular words** (p. 149) or **Irregular Words** (p. 150). Target the specific area of sound analysis needed.

Examples

1 | | | | Find the 2 sounds in the word **see**.

2 | ● | ● | | **Net** — when you find the **last** sound in your mouth put a counter on the last square. Say the whole word and feel the last sound come out of your mouth. What was it?

3 | | ● | | We want to find the **middle** sound — **sun**. Say **sun**. Now touch the squares as you break the word up into its sounds. When you touch the counter what sound is coming out of your mouth?
Repeat with words from same family — **run, fun,** and then others with the same middle sound — **rug**.

Note:

You can focus on long vowels in a similar way. Remember this is a activity so children are not required to spell the word. Valuable preparation for later reading and spelling is done at this talking and listening stage.

4 **How many sounds?**
Choose words (regular or irregular) from the words lists (pp. 149–150). Children fill in the **Grids** chart as they find the sounds in the given word and indicate how many sounds they found.
For example: for specific **blend listening**, listen for the last 2 sounds in **rust**.

| | | ? | ? |

Little Bits of Words 1

pear

two

saw

up

four

bee

Skill:	Analyzing the sounds in two-sounded words.
Teacher's Notes:	Say the words as a class. Announce that they each have two sounds in them. Have the children listen and feel the sounds in their mouth as they say the words and then put their fingers on the dots as each sound is found.
See also:	**Little Bits of Words 2** (p. 146), **Grids** (p. 148), **Regular Words** (p. 149) and **Irregular Words** (p. 150).
Extension:	Using the two-part grid (p. 166) the children find the two sounds in words read out by the teacher (see **Two-Sounded Words** in lists (pp. 149-150). Counters or blocks can be moved onto the grid as the sounds are said.

Little Bits of Words 2

ten ● ● ●

mat ● ● ●

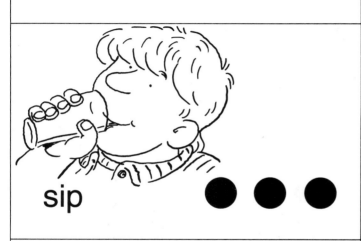

sip ● ● ●

lamp ● ● ● ●

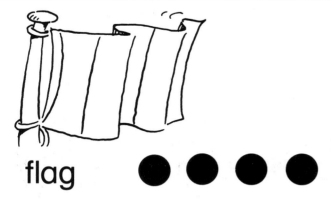

flag ● ● ● ●

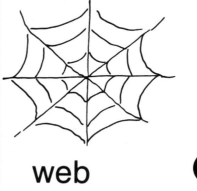

web ● ● ●

Skill:	Analyzing the sounds in three-and four-sounded words.
Teacher's Notes:	Say the words as a class. Announce that they each have three or four sounds in them. Have the children listen and feel the sounds in their mouth as they say the words and then put their fingers on the dots as each sound is found.
Extension:	On the back of this page children draw four pictures — drum, map, nest and face. After finding the sounds in the words, they draw the correct number of dots under the picture.

How Many Sounds?

1	●
2	● ●
3	● ● ●
4	● ● ● ●

Skill: Identifying the number of sounds in words.

Teacher's Notes: Each child has a copy of this page and uses it to indicate the number of sounds in words spoken by the teacher. The child can do this by placing counters on the appropriate line. If the sheet has been cut up into individual cards, the child can hold up the appropriate card instead.

See also: **Little Bits of Words 1** (p. 145), **Regular Words** (p. 149) and **Irregular Words** (p. 150).

1

1

2

1	2

3

1	2	3

4

1	2	3	4

Skill:	Analyzing sounds in words.
Teacher's Notes:	Children use counters or blocks in the appropriate grid to help them discover the sounds in words.
See also:	**Regular Words** (p. 149), **Irregular Words** (p. 150), **Keep It Concrete** (pp. 142-143) and **Feel and Find** (p. 144).

Regular Words

2 sounds = 2 letters
up   in   at   an   if   it   us

3 sounds = 3 letters

rat	jet	hit	not	nut
sat	net	fit	cot	but
van	den	pin	hot	gun
pan	pen	tin	fog	fun
tag	leg	fig	log	rug
wag	beg	jig	jog	bug
jam	hem	rim	mop	gum
ram	web	him	top	hum
sap	yes	sip	pop	cup
gap	vet	rip	box	pup
fax	let	fix	sox	rub
tax	men	mix	job	cub
mad	hen	lid	mob	mud
pad	led	hid	cob	bud

4 sounds = 4 letters

(blend at start)

stop	grip	skip
skin	glad	slap
snip	plot	clip
slot	prop	brag
swim	flag	grab
spin	frog	flat
crop	twin	trap
blot	clap	pram
brat	glum	slip

(blend at end)

lamp	felt	best
rust	mint	lend
hand	tusk	melt
help	silt	romp
desk	must	risk
lisp	hand	lost
band	cost	limp
mist	camp	runt
dusk	gulp	sent

5 sounds = 5 letters

crust	stilt	gland	lump	crimp	tramp
stamp	spent	grunt	brisk	trend	glint
cramp	smelt	twist	brand	slant	plant
print	frost	trust	crisp	flint	steps

149

Irregular Words

The number of letters does **not** equal the number of sounds.

1 sound

oh	ah	ear	our	eye

2 sounds

see	pear	fur	ape	ice	edge
zoo	shoe	knee	chew	why	earth
add	lie	off	neigh	owl	roar
far	toy	arch	bear	dough	they
paw	sour	saw	shear	tire	tear

3 sounds

knife	sheep	side	touch	feet
read	make	knock	rhyme	kneel
yell	lime	surf	rough	rope
pork	wash	fish	bike	nine
fight	hedge	lamb	phone	chop
fuss	toes	pouch	fall	foal
rain	soap	loud	thing	chin

4 sounds

cream	crane	soccer	mount	roast
plate	slope	poker	paste	paint
sniff	clues	cover	learned	found
blood	please	water		
brown	school	ruler	signed	sipped
skate	broom	measure	robbed	raked
train	croak	mother	bombed	hissed
preach	brain	hammer	hugged	laughed
green	flight		seized	washed
clown	spoke			

Skill: Identifying short vowels at the beginning of words.
Teacher's Notes: Children cut out the cards and say the names of the pictures. They are: apple, ink, elephant, orange, egg, umbrella, ant, under, octopus, empty, igloo, underwear. Ask children to draw their own pictures that begin with short vowels in the blank squares. What sounds do they start with? Using the **Short Vowel Cards (p. 43)**, match the picture to the letter for the sound.
See also: **Yes and No Cards** (p. 86) and **Find the Short Vowels** (p. 153).

Analysis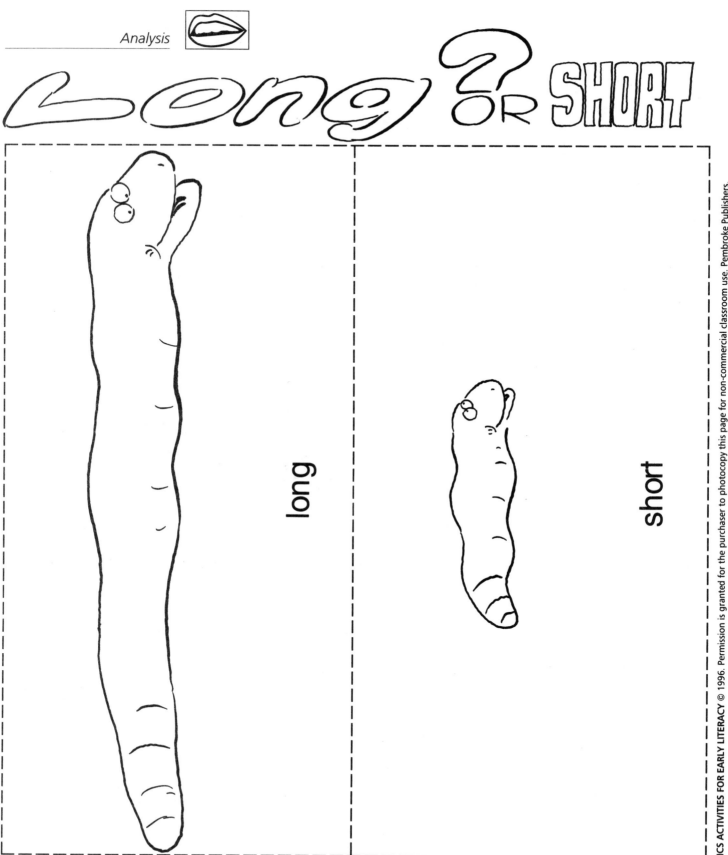

Long? OR SHORT

long

short

Skill: Recognizing long and short vowels.
Teacher's Notes: Children colour in the long and short worms and cut out the cards. Make sure that the children know which represents long and short so that they can match these with long and short vowels. Use these in conjunction with activities on (pp. 153-157).
See also: **Find the Short Vowels** (p. 153), **Long Vowels** (p. 154), **Long or Short Vowels?** (p. 155) and **Short/Long Vowel List** (p. 156).

Analysis

Find the Short Vowels: at the beginning of the word

- Say a word — choose from vowel categories randomly.
- Children repeat the word and **find** the sound at the beginning.
- They show their answer by
  1) saying the sound
  2) holding up the vowel card (see p. 43), or
  3) writing the letter for the chosen sound.

a	apple arrow acrobat ant and angry antiseptic agile acid aster abalone ash Ashleigh abracadabra absolutely
e	egg empty effort energy ethics every extra exit
i	in if imp igloo ink itch ill indefinite is it
o	octopus off on oscillate otter odd offer oleander ominous ox oxygen
u	up umbrella under utter uncle udder ugly unthinkable understand upstairs

153

Find the Long Vowels: at the beginning of words

- Say a word — choose from vowel categories randomly.
- Children repeat the word and find the **long** vowel sound at the beginning.
- They say their answer and repeat the initial **long** vowel.

Note: This is a listening activity — it does not matter that spelling of the long vowel varies.

a	Amy ace ape age agent ate acre aid aphid ale aim eight
e	eve eel easy each eat Eden even eager evening
i	ice ivy idle aisle ibis icon iris eiderdown eyes
o	open over oboe oak only overalls oats ogre ozone Owen oath
u	use useful unit utility unicorn ukulele

Long or Short Vowels?
• •

At the beginning of Words

- Use the lists of words beginning with:
  long vowels **short** vowels (p. 156).
- Choose words randomly and, after saying a word, ask the children to indicate whether the first sound they hear (vowel) is long or short.
- You may wish to use the 'worm' symbols for **long** and **short** (p.152).
- Children experiencing difficulty may find it helpful to run their finger along the worm as they say the word.
  For example:

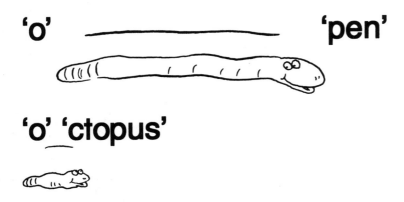

'o' ————————— **'pen'**

'o' 'ctopus'

In the Middle of Words

- Use the word list on page 156 which contrasts words with **short** and **long** vowels in the middle and continue the listening activity as above.

Short/Long Vowel List

a

add/aid	am/aim	can/cane
lad/laid	ran/rain	plan/plane
pad/paid	van/vain	fat/fate
mad/made	Gran/grain	mat/mate
pan/pain	bat/bait	
man/main	nap/nape	

e

Ben/been	wed/weed	set/seat
red/reed	bled/bleed	men/mean
fell/feel	bed/bead	peck/peak
step/steep	Ben/bean	speck/speak
fed/feed	best/beast	stem/steam
met/meet	net/neat	

i

sit/sight	lick/like	tip/type
mit/might	hick/hike	pill/pile
fit/fight	rip/ripe	till/tile
lit/light	whip/wipe	fill/file
	rid/ride	mill/mile

o

hop/hope	not/note	cot/coat
cop/cope	wok/woke	got/goat
mop/mope	rod/rode	sock/soak
pop/pope		

u

mull/mule
done/dune
mutt/mute
cut/cute

Short Vowel Search

Say the two words listed. Which one has the 'boxed' sound in the middle?

Children hold up the appropriate alphabet card.

For example: 'cap bed — Which has the 'e' sound in the middle?'
Answer **bed**.

'e'	cap	bed		'u'	cup	ran
'i'	pin	fan		'e'	red	sun
'o'	rot	cat		'i'	pip	pop
'a'	fun	back		'o'	bet	hop
'u'	nut	pat		'u'	cop	run
'i'	vet	nip		'a'	wet	cab
'a'	man	rob		'e'	fed	tan
'e'	Ben	bin		'i'	gun	sick
'o'	tub	cot		'g'	rub	van

Analysis

Likes to hide his 'r' sound in some words.

Skill: Identifying '**r**' in initial consonant blends.

Teacher's Notes: This activity, and the one on page 159, introduces children to blends. Say a word (using the contrasting words from the '**r**' blend word list, p. 172). If the child can hear Rolly's sound he or she places a tick or a counter in Rolly's box. If he or she cannot hear Rolly's sound then they place a tick or counter in the blank box.

See also: **Listening Corner** (p. 122) and **Initial Consonant Blend Word List** (p. 171).

Extension: Children look at their readers or favourite picture books. They copy down all the words they find which contain a '**r**' initial consonant blend.

158

Lucy the Lizard...

A SOUND WAY: PHONICS ACTIVITIES FOR EARLY LITERACY © 1996. Permission is granted for the purchaser to photocopy this page for non-commercial classroom use. Pembroke Publishers.

Likes to hide her 'l' sound in some words.

Skill:	Identifying 'l' in initial consonant blends.
Teacher's Notes:	Say a word (using the contrasting words from the 'l' blend word list, p. 171. If the child can hear Lucy's sound he or she places a tick or a counter in Lucy's box. If he or she cannot hear Lucy's sound then they place a tick or counter in the blank box.
See also:	**Listening Corner** (p. 122) and **Initial Consonant Blend Word List** (p. 171).
Extension:	Children write a sentence using four of the 'l' blend words.

159

First SOUND SNAP

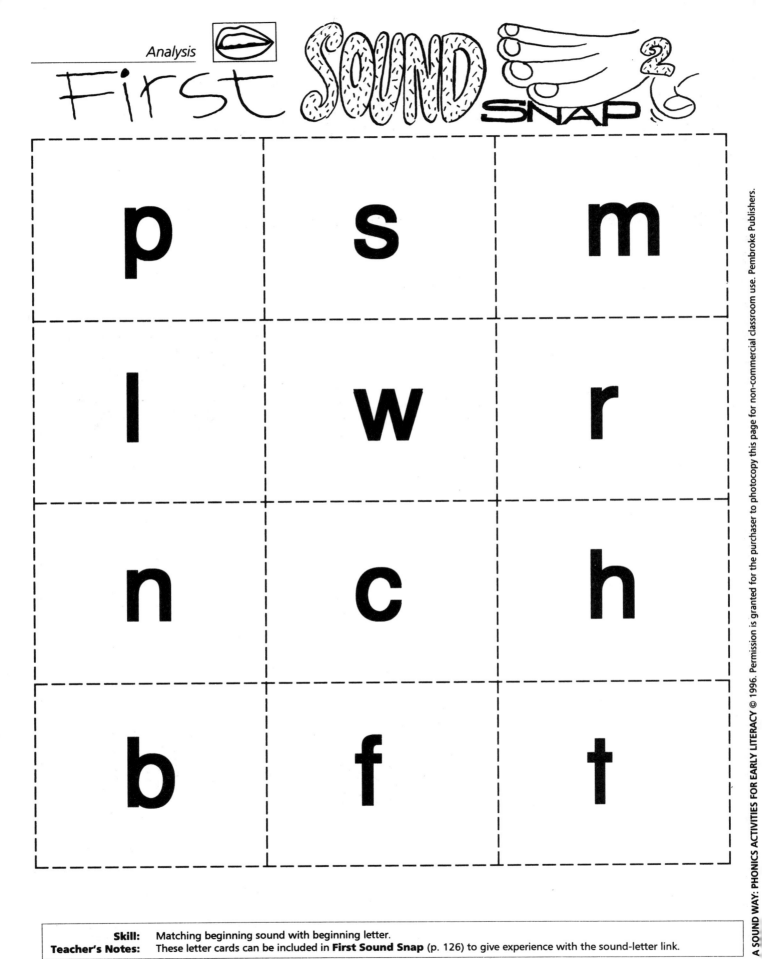

p	**s**	**m**
l	**w**	**r**
n	**c**	**h**
b	**f**	**t**

Skill: Matching beginning sound with beginning letter.
Teacher's Notes: These letter cards can be included in **First Sound Snap** (p. 126) to give experience with the sound-letter link.

Say the name of each picture.

Find the last sound in the name.

Write the letter for this sound under the picture.

A SOUND WAY: PHONICS ACTIVITIES FOR EARLY LITERACY © 1996. Permission is granted for the purchaser to photocopy this page for non-commercial classroom use. Pembroke Publishers.

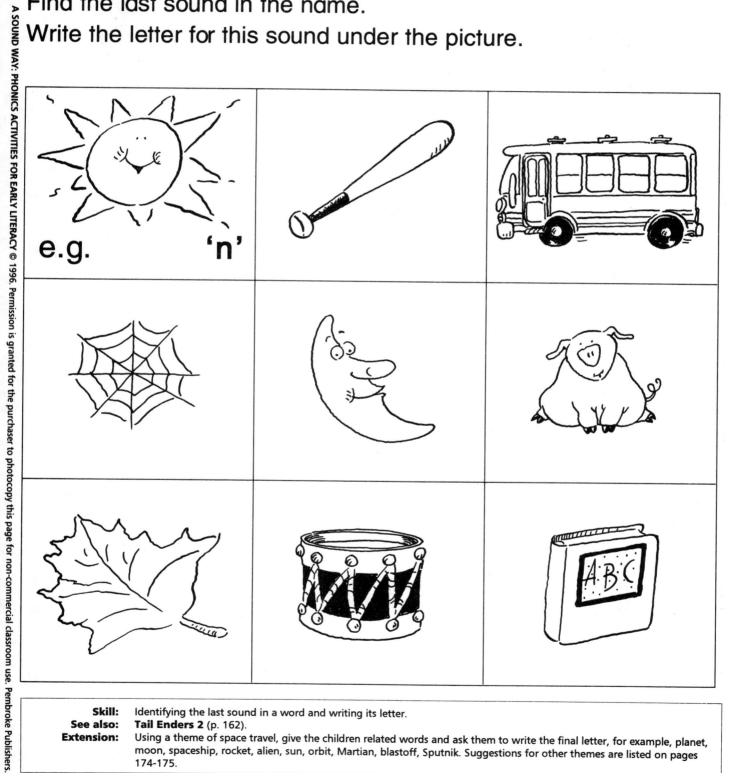

e.g.   'n'

Skill: Identifying the last sound in a word and writing its letter.
See also: **Tail Enders 2** (p. 162).
Extension: Using a theme of space travel, give the children related words and ask them to write the final letter, for example, planet, moon, spaceship, rocket, alien, sun, orbit, Martian, blastoff, Sputnik. Suggestions for other themes are listed on pages 174-175.

tail enders 2

Draw five animals that have tails in the space below.

What sound does the animal's name end with? For example,

Dog — 'g'.

Write the letter for this sound next to the animal.

A SOUND WAY: PHONICS ACTIVITIES FOR EARLY LITERACY © 1996. Permission is granted for the purchaser to photocopy this page for non-commercial classroom use. Pembroke Publishers.

Skill:	Identifying the last sound in a word.
See also:	**Tail Enders 1** (p. 161).
Extension:	Draw five animals. Exchange your drawings with a partner. On your partner's sheet, decide what sound comes at the end of the animal's name. Write the letter for this sound next to the animal.

Tic-Tac-Toe

Choose a game board. Cross off the letter that matches
the **last sound** you can hear in the words read by the teacher.
The first to get three crossed off in a row is the winner.

A SOUND WAY: PHONICS ACTIVITIES FOR EARLY LITERACY © 1996. Permission is granted for the purchaser to photocopy this page for non-commercial classroom use. Pembroke Publishers.

b	l	k
s	n	g
f	t	z

l	g	p
m	t	s
d	x	n

m	b	x
k	p	t
f	l	d

Skill:	Matching the last sound in a spoken word with a letter.
Teacher's Notes:	Choose words randomly from this list: red, boat, yes, box, rub, kick, bell, pig, sniff, kill, bad, peg, fox, bus, feel, seat, luck, ten, plan, tram, cuff, smell, hold, rip, fun, sand, bet, fold, tent, rock, tub, keep, fight, trim, top, puff, train, sock, met, read, steal, hand, rug, wet, can, sum, buzz.
Extension:	Children choose one group of letters from the game board on this page. Now rule up a blank **Tick-Tac-Toe** grid and draw pictures that end with these letters (sounds) in the blank squares.

SQUARE UP

Choose nine picture cards. Place or stick these in the large boxes provided. Say the word, find the sounds, then write the letters for these sounds in the small boxes.

A SOUND WAY: PHONICS ACTIVITIES FOR EARLY LITERACY © 1996. Permission is granted for the purchaser to photocopy this page for non-commercial classroom use. Pembroke Publishers.

Skill: Analyzing three-sounded words.
Teacher's Notes: Use **Three-Sounded Words A** (p. 183) for picture cards.
Extension: Children cut each card from top to bottom to make three pieces. Give these to a friend to reassemble by matching the picture and letter sequence.

Find the Sounds, then the Letters

• •

When children are competent at finding sounds in 2- and 3-sounded words and have mastered a number of sound-letter links, they can begin to spell words and use **Square Up** (page 164) and **Grid Worksheet** (page 166).

Suggestions:
- Use the words from the **Regular Words** (p. 149).
  - Indicate which grid to use (later children can be left to decide for themselves).
  - Say a word — children repeat it. For example: **cut**.
  - Ask the children to find the sounds in their mouths then write the letters in the squares. For example:

- Instead of writing the letters children may select letter squares and place them in order on the large grid (see page 148).

- Vary the above activity to incorporate skills of blending and manipulation. For example:
  'Rub out the **'t'** — what else could we put there? What word have we made?'
  'Change the **'u'** to **'o'**. What does it say now?'

- Pictures can be used as a stimulus for spelling — see **Three Sounded Words A** and **B** (p. 183 & 184) and **Square Up** (p. 164).

Note: Always be prepared to return to the use of counters or blocks to represent the sounds if the letters are causing confusion.

- **'sh', 'ch', 'th', 'ee', 'oo'** These are written in **one** square — one sound out of the mouth but we must write two letters or more, for example: **igh** in **ligh**t.

GRID Worksheet

2

3

4

Skill: Analyzing sounds within words.
See also: **Find the Sounds, then the Letters** (p. 165).

A SOUND WAY: PHONICS ACTIVITIES FOR EARLY LITERACY © 1996. Permission is granted for the purchaser to photocopy this page for non-commercial classroom use. Pembroke Publishers.

Sound Listening

Name each picture. Listen for the last sound in each word. Match the word with its picture.

tip	tim ✓	tick	bat	back	bag
pig	pin	pill	fish	fit	fin
mat	man	map	can	cat	cap
peg	pen	pet	doll	dot	dog

A SOUND WAY: PHONICS ACTIVITIES FOR EARLY LITERACY © 1996. Permission is granted for the purchaser to photocopy this page for non-commercial classroom use. Pembroke Publishers.

Skill: Analyzing final consonants.
Extension: Children choose three words then write each word in a sentence.

Say each word. Try to forget how they are spelled. Listen for how many sounds you can hear and write the number next to the word.

For example:

have(3)   **pet**(3)   **sold**(4)

plan( )	food( )	wish( )
stand( )	party( )	stop( )
win( )	thing( )	train( )
black( )	shop( )	big( )
chips( )	steps( )	book( )
crack( )	same( )	fitness( )
prove( )	this( )	within( )
form( )	old( )	needs( )
went( )	longer( )	judge( )
blind( )	happy( )	floor( )
street( )	shoot( )	scream( )

Skill: Counting the number of sounds in words.
See also: **Regular** and **Irregular word** lists (pp. 149–150).
Extension: In a small group, children hide one hand under a cloth. The leader or teacher calls out a word from the lists (pp. 149–150). Each child indicates the number of sounds in that word by extending their fingers under the cloth. When ready the cloth is removed and the correct answer is discussed.

A SOUND WAY: PHONICS ACTIVITIES FOR EARLY LITERACY © 1996. Permission is granted for the purchaser to photocopy this page for non-commercial classroom use. Pembroke Publishers.

HOW MANY SOUNDS/LETTERS?

When we say a word, the number of **sounds** we say is not always the same as the number of **letters** needed to write the same word. Say the names of the pictures. How many sounds? How many letters? Write your answers.

🌳	**3** sounds	**4** letters	
	_____ sounds	_____ letters	
	_____ sounds	_____ letters	
	_____ sounds	_____ letters	
	_____ sounds	_____ letters	
	_____ sounds	_____ letters	
	_____ sounds	_____ letters	

Skill: Identifying the number of sounds and letters in words.
Extension: Class activity — Using the following words as examples (shark, port, day, well, duck, happy, moth) use different colours to underline the letters making up the sounds in the word, for example, **sh-a-rk**.

169

Two sounds go together at the start of the names of the pictures below. Say the name and find the **first 2 sounds.** Now find the **2 letters** for these **2 sounds.** Draw a line from the letters to the picture.

Skill:	Identifying initial consonant blends.
Teacher's Notes:	Words on this page: clock, spoon, glass, flag, star, block, stroller, swan.
Extension:	Children brainstorm a list of '**tr**' and '**pr**' words, then write them on the back of this page. Up to 10 words — good, 15 words — excellent, 20+ words — sensational!

A SOUND WAY: PHONICS ACTIVITIES FOR EARLY LITERACY © 1996. Permission is granted for the purchaser to photocopy this page for non-commercial classroom use. Pembroke Publishers.

Initial Consonant Blend Word List

Use the following lists of words to introduce and analyze difficult initial consonant blends. Many children find it hard to discriminate the second sound in **s** blends or **'r'** and **'l'** in a consonant blend. For example: **smell, play, tree**.

Word pairs that provide a minimal sound contrast for these blends are listed. These should help the teacher select pairs of words for use with **Rolly Rabbit** and **Lucy Lizard** and other listening activities.

Children who have persistent difficulty locating the second sound may be helped by further word contrasts such as **bleed, lead, bead**.

Triple blends are even harder to hear and the teacher may need to use a framework for the number of sounds as described in **Keep it Concrete** (p. 142).

L Blends

pl	bl	cl
play / pay	black / back	clan / can
please / peas	blind / bind	clap / cap
plug / pug	blank / bank	clash / cash
plant / pant	blue / boo	clock / cock
plan / pan	bleat / beat	clog / cog
plus / pus	blow / bow	club / cub
plain / pain	bleed / bead	climb
plane / pane	blond / bond	cling
plop / pop	blew / boo	cliff
place / pace	bloom / boom	class
plough	blade / bade	clown
plate	block	clever

fl	gl	sl
flame / fame	glue / goo	slide / side
flat / fat	gloat / goat	slip / sip
floor / four / for	glory / gory	slap / sap
fly / fie	glad	slang / sang
flap	glass	slit / sit
flash	glimmer	slam / Sam
flick	gland	sleep / seep
flop	globe	slash / sash
flute	glove	slow / sow
float	glare	sling
flag	glide	slope

R Blends

pr
pray / pay
pram / Pam
prop / pop
private
princess
preen
prance / pants
prank
press

tr
tree / tea
trap / tap
trip / tip
truck / tuck
try / tie
trick / tick
true / too / to / two
trot / tot
train
tram

dr
dream / deem
drip / dip
dry / die
dray / day
drag / dag
drug / dug
drab / dab
drop

br
bride / bide
broom / boom
braid / bade
bread / bed
brought / bought
brand / band
brake / bake
bright / bite
brush

cr
crab / cab
creep / keep
crate / Kate
crop / cop
crumb / come
crash / cash
cry
cream
crazy

fr
Fred / fed
frog / fog
frame / fame
fry / fie
fright / fight
freight / fate
fresh
from
fruit

gr
great / gate
grape / gape
grab
green
grass
grin

str
street / seat
string / sing
stray / say
stroll
straight
stripe

scr
screen / seen
scream / seem
screech
scrape
scroll
scratch

spr
spring / sing
sprain / Spain
spree / see
sprite
sprang
spread

S Blends

sp

sport / sort
spy / sigh
spoil / soil
spank / sank
spoon / soon
spick / sick
spoil / soil
spill / sill
spun / sun
spat / sat
spoke / soak
spot
spin
spider

sm

smell / sell
smack / sack
smash / sash
smooth / soothe
stale / sale
smoke
smock / sock
smog
small
smile

st

steal / seal
stink / sink
stand / sand
sting / sing
stoop / soup
store / sore
still / sill
stack / sack
start
stop
stamp
stay

sn

sneer / seer
sneeze / seize
snap / sap
snail / sail
snake / sake

sw

swing / sing
sweep / seep
sweet / seat
swell / sell
swoon / soon

sk / sc

skip / sip
skill / sill
skite / site
skit / sit
skate

sl see **L Blends**

Initial Consonant Blends in Themes

The following lists of words containing initial consonant blends are arranged in themes. They are intended as a teacher resource for listening practice using words based around classroom themes and for inclusion in spelling lists. They can also be useful for activities where the children must listen to the word and write the initial consonant blend.

Workers in the community

driver	clerk	plumber	grocer	traffic officer	
grazier	florist	steward	professor	plasterer	cleaner

Countries

Switzerland	France	Scotland	Greece	Britain	Brazil
Spain	Scandinavia				
province	trade	treaty	traitor	flag	spy

Math

triangle	three	fraction	greater	protractor	process
graph	plus	square	group	product	scale

Shopping

spend	trolley	brand	brochure	groceries	brought

Transport

transport	travel	tram	train	trip	freight
plane	fly	station	glider	scooter	speedboat

Insects

fly	grub	spider	flea	grasshopper
sting	swarm	crawl	spray	dragonfly

Animals

crayfish	prawn	crab	crocodile	frog	platypus
stallion	spaniel	snake	grub	flamingo	stork
crow	swan	prance	sting	climb	stalk
slither	swim	growl	fly	snap	prowl

Home and family

grandma/grandmother		grandpa/grandfather	granny	brother
friend	twin	triplets	pram	cradle	playpen
breakfast	bride	groom	story	blanket	provide

174

School

student	sport	drama	staff	study	project
graduate	crayon	primary	class	grade	draw
print	story	trace	stamp	flag	practice
grammar	playground	truant	sketch	glue	prefect

Weather

cloud	cloudy	sky	snow	smog	steamy
frost	freezing	blow	blizzard	climate	tropical
flash	storm	clear	trickle	drizzle	drought

Fruit/vegetables/food

plum	strawberry	blackberry	grape	grapefruit	blueberry
fruit	fresh	flavour	spinach	broccoli	Brussels sprouts
spaghetti	spice	cream	crepe	frankfurt	snack

Space

planet	star	probe	gravity	sputnik	transmit
probe	spacesuit	spaceship	transit	space	splashdown

Music

flute	trumpet	trombone	clarinet	drum	triangle
French horn	treble clef	clang	gramophone		stereo

Tools

spanner	broom	drill	spade	screwdriver	pliers

Health and Body

skin	skeleton	spine	skull	stomach	brain
throat	gland	plasma	specimen	pregnant	protein
sleep	breath	smell	drug	prescribe	stamina

Actions

climb	crawl	swim	twirl	skate	crouch
throw	skip	stand	stretch	smile	smoke
sneeze	sneer	sneak	glare	glance	flick
fly	float	spurt	spin	plunge	play
grab	groan	grumble	grin	grunt	drive
draw	drag	pry	fry	crackle	creak

S at the Start!

But what's next?

Listen for the second sound as you say these words — the sound straight after the 's'. Match this sound with a letter from the circle and then write the letter in the space provided.

e.g. snail

sn

t n m l
k w p

s __

s __

s __

s __

s __

s __

s __

s __

s __

Skill: Identifying the second sound in an initial consonant blend.
Extension: Children use three of the words from the pictures and write a True or False sentence for each, for example, 'You play with a snake.' T or F.

Look at the pictures. Say the words. Find the first two sounds and write the corresponding letters in the boxes to complete the word.

e.g.

b	r	oo	m

		a	n	t

		o	ss

		a	ck

		oo	n

		a	sh

		ai	n

		a	b

Skill: Identifying the two sounds in an initial consonant blend.
Extension: Using the blends from above, children write another word that begins with the same consonant blend, for example, broom—br—brave.

Make up a name — first name, middle name and surname — using the three letters in the numberplates below.

For example:

| PAD 006 | **Peter Alexander Deery** |

| FRS 222 | _____ |

| SEW 944 | _____ |

| TMR 767 | _____ |

| KJL 911 | _____ |

| SJB 521 | _____ |

| RBW 942 | _____ |

| JIM 210 | _____ |

Skill: Writing names that begin with a given capital letter.
Extension: Children draw a car with their own initials on the numberplate.

Make up a sentence of three words using each of the letters in the numberplates below. They can be as silly as you like!

For example:

EAL 024	**Emily ate leeches.**
PSC 874	_____
JDP 212	_____
KTM 303	_____
RBF 921	_____
HVW 111	_____
SLR 037	_____

Skill: Writing sentences using first-sound/letter knowledge.
Extension: Be creative. Make up a numberplate suitable for a teacher, an artist, a footballer, a dentist, a hairdresser, for example, Jane teaches lessons = JTL 551.

Find the Word

Choose a theme such as animals, body parts or names.
Write words (with or without pictures) associated with this theme on an 'answer sheet'.

Provide children with a series of charts of numbered blank squares corresponding to the number of letters in your chosen group of words. For example:

1	2	3	4	5	6	7

octopus

1	2	3

eel

Taking each letter in turn, give sound analysis tasks as clues.
These tasks can be of one type (e.g. listening for first sound) or a mixture of analysis skills.
For example: **eel**
1   the first sound in **edge**
2   the middle sound in **pen**
3   the second sound in **slow**

Note: This activity combines skills of sound analysis with practice in linking sounds and letters and gives opportunities for whole word identification.

Blending

This section encourages word discovery by getting children to listen to the individual sounds of a word then to blend them together to say the word.

Children often have difficulty blending the sounds they say themselves and it is for this reason that we have included the **Blending** section <u>after</u> the **Analysis** section.

As with analysis, children are encouraged to use concrete materials to represent component sounds and accompany their blending attempts with physical movement.

A segment on nonsense adds an element of fun while providing clear information about the children's skill level.

B-l-e-n-d-i-n-g

● ●

Using Pictures

See pp. 183–184, **Three-Sounded Words A** and **Three-Sounded Words B**.

Use whole or part of the **Three-Sounded Words** sheets or 'cut and paste' the individual pictures to make cards.

Call out a chosen word breaking it up into its individual sounds.

Children listen, say the discovered word and then place a counter on the picture of that word.

Alternatively, pictures could be cut out and given to a small group of children. Duplicates are placed in a container and drawn out by the teacher (or chosen child) to give as a blending task, e.g. '**sh**'–'**ee**'–'**p**'

The child who has that picture places it face up in a central position, after blending the sounds to identify the word. The 'winner' is the first person to have all his/her cards face up.

Using Words From Lists of 2, 3 & 4 Sounds

See **Regular** (p. 149) and **Irregular** (p. 150).

Present words orally for children to blend, such as '**sh**'–'**ee**' = **she**

A physical body movement such as moving arms from a stretched out position to meet in the midline may assist blending.

Similarly, counters or blocks can be used to represent the component sounds and then children push these together as they try to blend the sounds. See **Keep it Concrete** (p. 142).

Give meaning cues to children who are still experiencing difficulty.

Using Meaning Cues

Saying the word to be blended in a sentence provides meaning and grammatical cues to help the child select the appropriate word. For example: 'I hurt part of my foot — my '**t**'–'**oe**''.

Make sure you repeat the blending task for these words without using the meaning cue.

- Children can work in pairs or small groups to analyze and blend words for each other. (They can use the pictures on pp. 183, 184 or choose words from the list on p. 149.)
- When you give the sounds for the word to be blended, it is wise to encourage the children to imitate the individual sounds before blending them to make the whole word.

 *Blending*

Three-Sounded Words A

short medial vowels: regular spelling

Skill:	Identifying the sounds in regular three-sounded words.
Teacher's Notes:	Words on this page: hat, pin, jug, can, fox, bug, cat, box, bed, sun, ten, wig, fan, pen, cap, bus, pig, cup, dog, log. For example, three sounds = three letters. See p. 182 for activities.
See also:	**Square Up** (p. 164), **Find the Sounds, then the Letters** (p. 165), **Blending** (p. 182), **Three-Sounded Words B** (p. 184).

Blending

3-Sounded Words B

long medial vowels: irregular spelling

Geelong 2

A SOUND WAY: PHONICS ACTIVITIES FOR EARLY LITERACY © 1996. Permission is granted for the purchaser to photocopy this page for non-commercial classroom use. Pembroke Publishers.

Skill:	Identifying the sounds in irregular three-sounded words.
Teacher's Notes:	Words on this page: fork, ball, seat, horse, phone, boat, rake, sign, shape, face, bird, cart, knife, cork, coat, heart, sheep, case, nail, kite. See p. 182 for activities.
See also:	**Square Up** (p. 164), **Find the Sounds, then the Letters** (p. 165), **Blending** (p. 182), **Three-Sounded Words A** (p. 183).

A Place for Nonsense

A SOUND WAY: PHONICS ACTIVITIES FOR EARLY LITERACY © 1996. Permission is granted for the purchaser to photocopy this page for non-commercial classroom use. Pembroke Publishers.

- Children's performance with nonsense word tasks will reveal how firmly they have grasped the various aspects of Phonological Awareness.
- Using nonsense also encourages children to 'have a go' at tasks which they might otherwise judge as only suitable for much younger children.

Blending

- Introduce the activity imaginatively. For example: I know a family of 'ipets' who live underground. They had fifty babies last week and each baby has a different name. You find the name by putting together the two sounds I give you.

  'e'–'t', 'o'–'j', 's'–'u', 'm'–'i', 'ee'–'p', 'ar'–'d', 'l'–'oy', 'f' 'igh' etc.

- Extend this activity to 3– and 4–sounded words. For example: Last year's baby 'ipets' names have three-sounds each. Listen and find their names.

  'r'–'o'–'j', 'n'–'e'–'p', 'l'–'o'-'f', 'm'–'ay'–'g', 's'–'oy'–'d', 'r'–'igh'–'v'

The use of counters, blocks etc. may be helpful (see page 182).

Analysis

- Introduce the activity imaginatively. For example: 'Gozzers' live high up in the trees — they are so small we can't see them but we can hear their names. All their names have two sounds — say the name after me and then tell me what the sounds are in it. (You could also ask for the first or last sound.)

  'om', 'ab', 'et', 'di', 'lu', 'tor', 'sair', 'oyb'

- Extend this exercise to 3- or 4-sounded nonsense words — perhaps for the names of all the older 'Gozzers'. Use a grid or counters to give a framework for analyzing particular sound positions.

Blending

Use letter tiles or cards (as described on page 143) that have vowels one colour and consonants another. Choose combinations of letters. For example:

> vowel + consonant   2-sounded word
> consonant + vowel   2-sounded word
> or 3-sounded word — 'c' + 'v' + 'c'.

Say the sound sequence and blend to form 'name', or a nonsense language word.

Analysis

- Children listen to a nonsense word, find the sounds as they repeat the word and then write the letter equivalents for those sounds.
  Accept variations in the choice of letters which represent the sounds.

For example:

| o | s | or | o | ss | , | u | ck | or | u | k |

Proceed to 3- and 4-sounded words, with tasks varying from analysis of initial, medial, final (2nd or 2nd last — these involve blends) to finding all the sounds in the word.

Choose and Change

• •

Once children have established the letter–sound link of five consonants and three vowels, show them how these can be manipulated in words.

Choose three-letter, phonically regular words and write the letters for the **middle** and **last** sounds in the second and third solid boxes on (p. 188) e.g. **'at'**, **'an'**, **'in'**. Letter tiles for **p, t, b, m, r, f** can be placed in the perforated boxes and then, in turn, placed in the first solid box to form a word.

Children should say the sound as they place the letter tile.

Suggested dialogue:

These two letters say **at**.
Put letter **p** in the first box, and say its sound.
Now what does the word say? **pat** — **'p'-'at'**.
Now take away the letter **p** and replace it with letter **m**, say its sound.
Now what does the new word say? **mat** — **'m'-'at'**.
Continue with other letters and encourage the children to experiment with first letter choices to form their own words.

- The same procedure can be adapted to emphasize final sound–letter links by adding and replacing letters in the third solid box. For example: **'ba'-'t'**, **'ba'-'n'**.

- It can be extended further to demonstrate the way words change when the middle letter is replaced (short vowel).
  'b'-'a'-'t' → **'b'-'i'-'t'** → **'b'-'u'-'t'**.

Extension: Provide the children with the letter tiles and page 188. Write **at** in the second and third boxes. Ask them to add a letter to make the word say **pat** or **mat** or **cat**.

Choose and Change

Skill: Manipulating sounds in words.
Teacher's Notes: Activities (p. 187).

Skill:	Identifying sound families in written words.
Teacher's Notes:	This activity introduces students to word families.
See also:	Instructions, **Visiting the Family** (pp. 190–191).
Extension:	Children draw four members of the imaginary '**et**', '**ing**' or '**ot**' family and give them all names.

Visiting the Family

Some suggestions about how to work with word families. (Use with p. 189)

Reading

- Choose a stem or ending like **at**, **ust** or **id**.
- Write it in the roof of the house, for example: **at**.
- The family then becomes the '**at**' family.
- Write words on the steps, for example:

   cat   **flat**
   mat   **spat**
   bat

These words may vary depending on the level of difficulty required.
- You can leave spaces for children to either, copy, write and say your word, or think of other words. More than one word can go on a step.
- Children say the words as they go up the steps to visit the family. They can say them again as they leave!

Listening

- Does . . . belong with this family?
- Children have two or more houses, such as **-it** family and **-ick** family. Ask where does '**sick**' belong?
- Contrast easily confused groups like **-ed** and **-end**.

Spelling

- Children write given or self-selected words on the steps.
- Encourage them to say the words slowly and find the sounds.

Some suggested 'Families'
(use with pp. 189 and 190)

-od pod cod	**-ob** rob lob	**-og** dog log	**-op** top cop	**-ox** box fox	**-ot** cot not
-ug rug tug	**-ub** rub cub	**-um** rum hum	**-un** fun run	**-up** cup pup	**-ut** nut hut
-et pet net	**-en** ten men	**-ed** red bed	**-eg** peg leg	**-ix** fix six	**-im** him Tim
-it sit lit	**-id** lid rid	**-in** bin pin	**-ig** big fig	**-ib** bib nib	**-ip** tip nip
-at rat fat	**-ag** rag lag	**-an** ban ran	**-am** ram Sam	**-ap** cap tap	**-ad** mad sad
-amp ramp camp	**-elt** felt belt	**-ump** rump lump	**-imp** limp	**-omp** romp	Don't forget the 'spelling rule' families! e.g. **ee** **ar** etc.
-and sand band	**-end** bend mend	**-ust** rust dust	**-ind** wind rind	**-olt** colt bolt	
-ant pant	**-ent** bent went		**-int** mint lint	**-old** gold bold	
	-est test west		**-ist** mist fist		**plural** -ts -gs etc.

Say the sound for the letter in each of the boxes.
Join them to make a word. Find the word in one of the bubbles.
Read the word quickly to pop it!

a	t
i	n
o	n
u	p
i	f
e	gg
u	s
o	ff
i	t
a	n

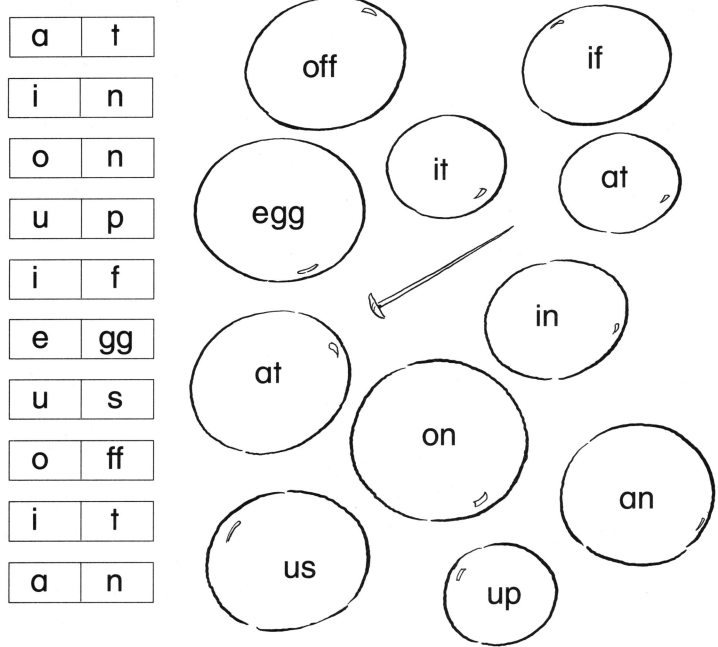

Skill:	Blending two-sounded words from letters.
Extension:	Write simple sentences on the board leaving a blank for a two-letter word. Read a sentence to the children and have them decide which of the two-letter words should fill the space. For example, 'Please come ———.' Write the word in the gap.

192

A SOUND WAY: PHONICS ACTIVITIES FOR EARLY LITERACY © 1996. Permission is granted for the purchaser to photocopy this page for non-commercial classroom use. Pembroke Publishers.

Blast off 1

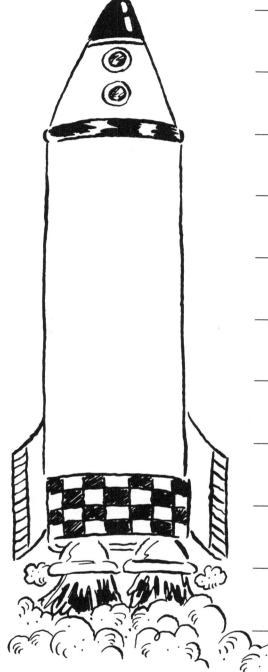

fun	10
hop	9
jig	8
rat	7
mad	6
net	5
tin	4
bus	3
cut	2
fed	1

10	sun
9	lip
8	fat
7	red
6	dad
5	hot
4	pin
3	man
2	pig
1	hum

Read the ten words as quickly as you can to launch the rocket.
Try again with the other ten words.

Skill:	Reading regular three-sound/three-letter words by sight or using the blending strategy.
Extension:	Children play this as a game with a partner. Using a 1–2 spinner or the heads and tails of a coin, they move their counters down the numbers 10–1 (BLAST OFF) saying the words as they move each turn. The first to reach 1 is the winner.

193

Have fun saying these nonsense words.

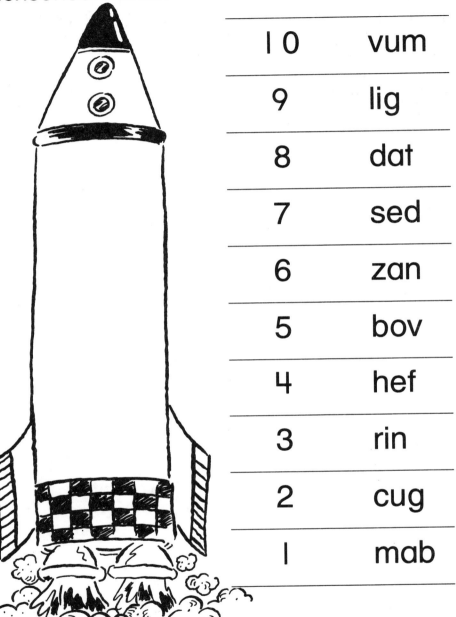

jed	10
zim	9
gop	8
cin	7
san	6
deg	5
boz	4
fut	3
las	2
rab	1

10	vum
9	lig
8	dat
7	sed
6	zan
5	bov
4	hef
3	rin
2	cug
1	mab

Read the ten words as quickly as you can to launch the rocket.
Try again with the other ten words.

A SOUND WAY: PHONICS ACTIVITIES FOR EARLY LITERACY © 1996. Permission is granted for the purchaser to photocopy this page for non-commercial classroom use. Pembroke Publishers.

Skill:	Reading nonsense three-sounded words by using the blending strategy.
See also:	**Blast Off 1** (p. 193).
Extension:	Children draw their own rocket ship and write 10 'real' three-sounded words on it.

Use letters from the rectangle to add a 'tail' to these word beginnings so that **real** words are made.
For example: **'bi'**–**'t'** = **bit**

Write your list on a separate piece of paper.

bi . . .

lo . . .

sa . . .

pe . . .

mu . . .

t   ck

ll   p

n

g   m

sh   b

d

x   ng

A SOUND WAY: PHONICS ACTIVITIES FOR EARLY LITERACY © 1996. Permission is granted for the purchaser to photocopy this page for non-commercial classroom use. Pembroke Publishers.

Skill: Blending word stems with different endings to create new words.
Extension: Children write five different 'tails' for this word beginning: **ca-**.

Blending

Head-Ons

Choose letters from the box and add them to the front of the word endings to make real words.

Write your list on a separate piece of paper.

p
t
m
f
s g
c
d

...op

...ed

...ig

...at

...an

...ug

Skill:	Blending initial sounds with ending word stems to create new words.
See also:	word family lists (p. 191).
Extension:	Write the individual letters on coloured cards (including new letters **h**, **b** and **r**). Write the endings on different coloured cards. Children mix and match the cards to make new words.

A SOUND WAY: PHONICS ACTIVITIES FOR EARLY LITERACY © 1996. Permission is granted for the purchaser to photocopy this page for non-commercial classroom use. Pembroke Publishers.

Flight Path

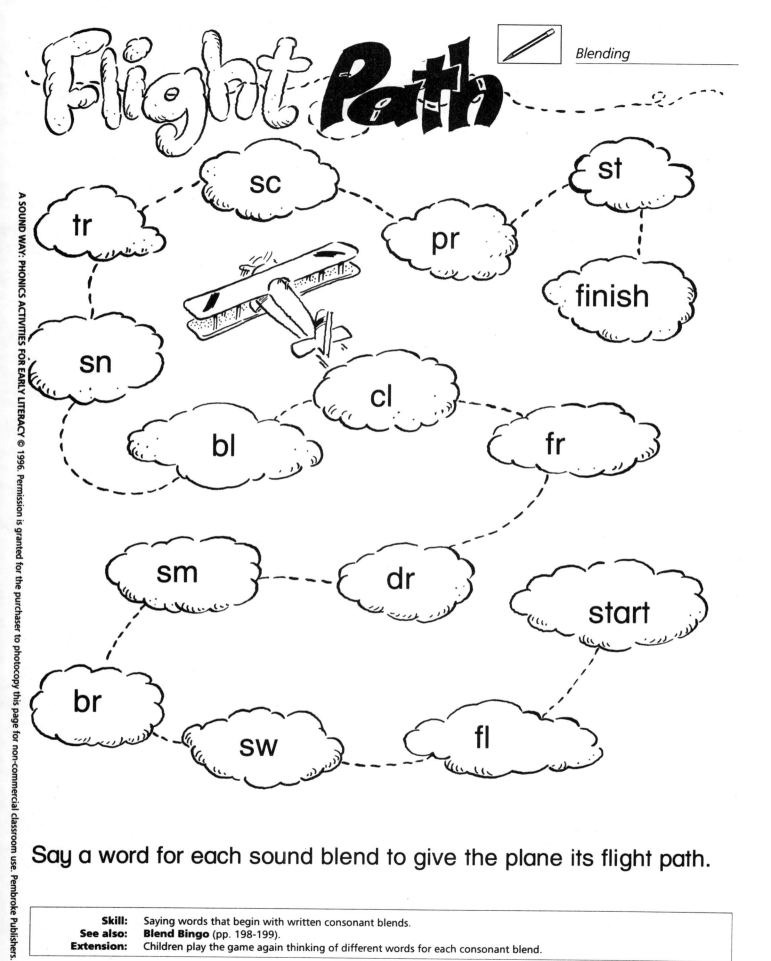

Say a word for each sound blend to give the plane its flight path.

Skill:	Saying words that begin with written consonant blends.
See also:	**Blend Bingo** (pp. 198-199).
Extension:	Children play the game again thinking of different words for each consonant blend.

Blend Bingo

cl	fl	gr	fr	sp
br	tr	sk	st	sm
pr	sl	fr	tw	cr
bl	sp	fl	pr	sc
sn	cl	sw	bl	dr
gl	dr	st	cr	pl

Skill: Identifying spoken initial consonant blends and matching them to letters.
See also: **Instructions** (p. 199), **Word Lists** (p. 199).
Extension: Children draw a ladder and on each rung write a word that begins with a consonant blend.

Blend Bingo

(Use with **Blend Bingo** p. 198.)

pram	twins	friend	play
spin	cry	stick	star
sleep	brown	clean	train
clap	spoon	flag	stick
sky	blue	swing	green
snail	stop	glad	smile
black	dress	plant	Frank
fly	scared	prize	climb
sneeze	blanket	stand	dream
crayon	glue	please	

Read words in random order. Student is to identify the initial sound blend and cover the appropriate letter blend.

Winner is the first to cover four in one row. Check off words as they are spoken and check the winning student's board.

Manipulation

Manipulation is the most difficult area of phonological awareness. It assumes competence in the areas of analysis and blending of sounds.

Manipulation tasks involve moving the sounds within words, removing a sound or replacing one sound with another sound to form a new word.

Some tasks can be done orally while in others the written letters provide support as the sounds they represent are changed or moved. Spelling rules are highlighted further in this section.

Sound Deletion

'What would **feet** say if we took away '**ff**'?'
Continue with each of the following words deleting the **first sound.**
Repeat the process deleting the **final sound**.
The words are: feet, boat, cart, think, call, bend, shelf
Note: **bend** and **shelf** are more difficult because they contain final
consonant blends. Use pictures to prompt if necessary.

Sound Deletion 1

The following word sequences provide sound deletion practice.
For example:

Say **feet**, what would it say without the '**f**'?
Say **feet**, what would it say without the '**t**'?

Base Word	First Sound Deletion	Last Sound Deletion
fee**t**	eet (eat)	fee
boa**t**	oat	boa (bow)
car**t**	art	car
thin**k**	ink	thing
cal**l**	all	ca (caw)
ben**d**	end	Ben
shel**f**	elf	shel (shell)
sea**t**	eat	sea
toa**d**	oad (ode)	toa (toe)
ban**d**	and	ban
sai**l**	ail	sai (say)
mat**e**	ate	ma (may)
mea**l**	eal (eel)	me

Sound Deletion 2

The following word sequences provide sound deletion practice within **consonant blends**.

Initial blend — **First sound** deletion. For example: Say **clap**. What would it say without the 'c'?

Initial blend — **Second sound** deletion. For example: Say **clap**. What would it say without the 'l'?

Base Word	First Sound Deletion	Second Sound Deletion
clap	lap	cap
try	ry (rye)	ty (tie)
play	lay	pay
trip	rip	tip
flit	lit	fit
twit	wit	tit
bread	read	bead (bed)
snip	nip	sip
blob	lob	bob
flow	low	fow (foe)
slap	lap	sap
trip	tip	rip

Note: These **Sound Deletion** activities are helpful for children who can read and write, but who may need extra practice with spelling.

Sound Deletion 3

The following word sequences provide sound deletion practice within consonant blends.
Final blend — **last sound** deletion. For example:
Say **bend**. What would it say without the '**d**'?
Final blend — **second last sound** deletion. For example:
Say **bend**. What would it say without the '**n**'?

Base Word	Last sound deletion	Second last deletion
bend	ben	bed
lost	los (loss)	lot
lamp	lam (lamb)	lap
bank	ban	bak (back)
rust	rus (Russ)	rut
went	wen (when)	wet
wild	wil (while)	wid (wide)
ramp	ram	rap
pant	pan	pat
hunt		hut
hand		had

CHANGE

Play this game with a friend.

Choose a word with three letters.

Take turns either: • adding one letter
  • removing one letter
  • changing one letter.

e.g.   cat bat bit hit hot

How long is your chain of words?

*   Use the back of this page for more space!

Skill:	Rearranging letters within words to form new words.
Extension:	Children play **word chain** orally in a small group or pairs. One child starts the chain by saying a word. For younger players, the next child must say a word that starts with the last sound of the previous word, for example, **bed—dog—gate—ten—needle—lake**. Older players must say a word that begins with the final letter of the previous word, for example, **ride—egg—gap—pinch—help**.

205

Letter Tricks 1

Change **fan** to **man**

e.g.

 fan   to    man

Clue: Either change one letter or rearrange the letters to make the new words. Try these!

bag	to	_____
run	to	_____
cat	to	_____
lap	to	_____
pen	to	_____
pat	to	_____
top	to	_____

Skill: Changing letters to make new words.
Teacher's Notes: Third drawing down on right column represents 'cot'. **Letter Tricks 1**, **2** and **3** (pages 209 and 210) can be used as spelling exercises.
Extension: Children solve riddles. For example, change '**p**' to '**b**', '**j**' to '**i**', '**r**' to '**z**', '**m**' to '**g**' and '**v**' to '**t**'.
Whav js plack and mold and moes pur, pur, pur? A pee flyjng packwards.

 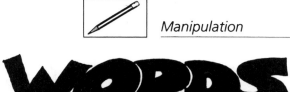

Can you rearrange the letters in these words to make a new word? Write your new word next to the arrow.

e.g. **ten** → **net**

pan →	on →
tub →	gum →
posh →	tug →
top →	pit →
nit →	tap →
bin →	pin →
pot →	tab →
mad →	dab →

Skill: Rearranging letters to form new words.
Extension: Can children think of any words or names that are the same spelt backwards or forwards? For example, bib, Anna.

Use the letters in the wheels to make as many words as you can.

For example:

pot   rat   port   part   tap   top   rot

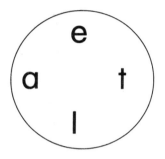

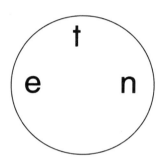

_____

_____

_____

_____

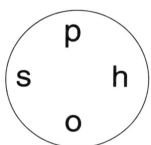

_____

_____

_____

_____

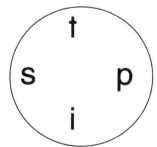

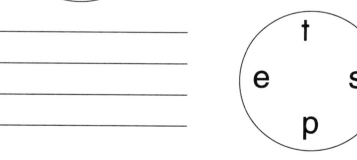

_____

_____

_____

_____

_____

_____

_____

_____

_____

Skill: Forming words by rearranging letters.
See also: **Letter Tricks 2** and **Letter Tricks 3** (pp. 209–210).
Extension: Give children the following words on a simple crossword grid, ten squares by ten squares. (nest, send, sad, star, rope, open, no, taps, bus, cub.) Can they fit them all in the crossword?

A SOUND WAY: PHONICS ACTIVITIES FOR EARLY LITERACY © 1996. Permission is granted for the purchaser to photocopy this page for non-commercial classroom use. Pembroke Publishers.

Letter Tricks 2

Manipulation

Change:

e.g.  train _____ to  rain _____

Clue: Add, delete, or rearrange the letters.

Now create your own **Letter Tricks.** Draw pictures to go with them below. Exchange them with a partner to complete the activity.

 _____ to _____ _____

_____ to _____ _____

_____ to _____ _____

Skill:	Changing letters to form new words.
Extension:	**Letter Tricks 1** and **Letter Tricks 3** (pp. 206 and 210).

Letter Tricks 3

Change:

e.g. man to  mane

Clue: Add or delete a letter.

 Tim to  _____

 cape to  _____

pip to  _____

tub to  _____

wine to _____

cane to _____

 cub to _____

Skill: Changing letters to form new words.
See also: **Letter Tricks 1** and **Letter Tricks 2** (pp. 206 & 209).
Extension: As a class, discuss the changes that were made. What spelling rule have you discovered?

More JUMBLED WORDS

Rearrange the letters in these words to make a new word. Write your new word next to the arrow.

e.g. shut → huts

step	→	stun	→
lame	→	nest	→
nips	→	slip	→
felt	→	post	→
silt	→	life	→
snail	→	meat	→
tame	→	seal	→

Make up your own jumbled words here.

Skill: Manipulating letters to make new words.
Extension: Cut up these words to make cards and use them in a board game. At each roll of the dice, the player must make a word from the letter jumble using all the letters on that card.

Tricky Triangles

Complete the triangles. Add or take away one letter from each row to make a new word. The first one has been done for you.

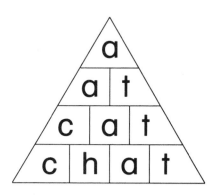

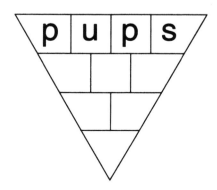

Use these blanks to make your own 'tricky triangles'.

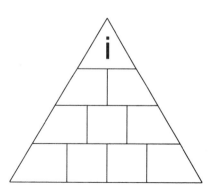

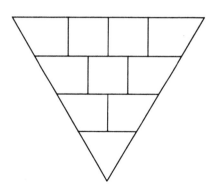

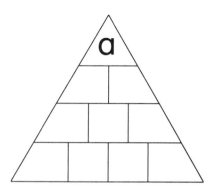

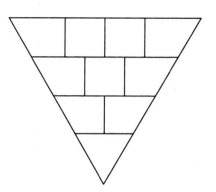

Skill: Adding and deleting letters to form words.

Brainstorming

How many smaller words can you find in the word **BRAINSTORMING** by rearranging the letters?

A SOUND WAY: PHONICS ACTIVITIES FOR EARLY LITERACY © 1996. Permission is granted for the purchaser to photocopy this page for non-commercial classroom use. Pembroke Publishers.

_____

_____

_____

_____

_____

_____

_____

_____

_____

20 words = good, 30 = excellent, 30+ = Ace!

Skill: Forming words from given letters.
Extension: Try a similar activity by brainstorming on the words: **unfortunately**, **Constantinople** and **hippopotamus**.

Are these words **real**, **possible** or **impossible**?

Write an **R**, **P** or **I** next to the word.

ptin	pson
step	gnu
plok	ratc
kept	riyz
sneck	betton
phyd	anqe
rekt	quan
pnose	hwear
stpable	bext
sbat	stroored

Skill: Learning about letter patterns that can and cannot occur in the English language.

A SOUND WAY: PHONICS ACTIVITIES FOR EARLY LITERACY © 1996. Permission is granted for the purchaser to photocopy this page for non-commercial classroom use. Pembroke Publishers.

BE A DETECTIVE

The trees in the playground have been trampled! Read the clues and solve the mystery of who did all the damage.

When you have your answer, draw it on the back of this page. (The first clue has been solved for you.)

1	silent letter at the end of [comb image]	**B**
2	second letter in the part of arm where a [watch image] goes.	
3	twice in [foot image] but never in [feet image]	
4	the letter after the silent one in [bow image]	
5	third letter in [kite image] and twice in [envelope image]	
6	second letter in the eleventh month of the year	
7	two numbers between 5 and 10 begin with this letter	
8	first letter of the alphabet	
9	first in [umbrella image] and in the middle of [cup image]	
10	twice in [cherries image]	
11	begins both [apple image] and [ant image]	
12	third letter in [fish image] and last in [bus image]	

A SOUND WAY: PHONICS ACTIVITIES FOR EARLY LITERACY © 1996. Permission is granted for the purchaser to photocopy this page for non-commercial classroom use. Pembroke Publishers.

Skill: Thinking about letters in words and using them to solve a puzzle.
Extension: Children make up their own puzzle for a friend.

215

Metalinguistic Trivia 1

Which one does not belong?
(This exercise can be done orally with a group or single student.)

1   ball beach sister band
2   fall small hall went
3   top hop mop flop ran
4   silly fix football fan
5   fly flag flap fish
6   post roast fold rest
7   lolly Sally falling bend
8   window toothache sun footpath
9   cup cut can cub
10 smash snake sneeze sneaky
11 farm start Mark mess
12 sunlight moonlight lighthouse starlight
13 tree train traffic tight
14 sold fold hold bolt
15 gorilla candle catch can

Manipulation

Metalinguistic Trivia 2

What do all these words have in common?

1	bat fat cat rat	**9**	bell well tell sell
2	single celery city Saturday	**10**	leg lake lady lesson
3	cap bad ran mat	**11**	jump jelly juice giant
4	pin fan den sun	**12**	carport sunshine shoelace night-time
5	sun rut cup tub	**13**	ripe arrow ready caravan
6	lamb knee wrong	**14**	tent pip Bob dead
7	sleep slide slow sling	**15**	kiss case grass lace
8	bend hand find pond		

Metalinguistic Trivia 3

What do all these words have in common?

1	fruit fresh Friday Frank	**9**	coconut telephone computer Saturday
2	stand pasta presto last	**10**	ant antics participant reliant
3	sister letter jumper mother	**11**	last car laugh
4	report important shorten torn	**12**	who how Harry heaven
5	invisible confidently satisfaction	**13**	when what why where
6	inside inform inner instruct	**14**	investigation magnificently alphabetical
7	finger photo Phoebe fish	**15**	eat ate tea
8	plan flower blow slope		

Metalinguistic Trivia Answers

Exercise 1 (p. 216) is the easiest of the three. It involves recognizing one word in the list which doesn't belong. Exercises 2 and 3 (p. 217) ask for recognition of a common attribute.

Answers

1

1 **sister** does not start with '**b**'.
2 **went** does not rhyme with **fall, small, hall**.
3 **ran** does not rhyme with **top, hop, mop, flop**.
4 **silly** does not start with '**f**'.
5 **fish** does not start with '**fl**' blend.
6 **fold** does not end with '**st**' blend.
7 **bend** does not contain '**l**'.
8 **sun** is not a two-syllable word.
9 **can** does not contain short vowel '**u**'.
10 **smash** does not start with '**sn**' blend.
11 **mess** does not contain '**ar**' vowel.
12 **lighthouse** does not have **light** as second part of the compound word.
13 **tight** does not start with '**tr**' blend.
14 **bolt** does not rhyme with **sold, fold, hold**.
15 **gorilla** does not start with '**c**'.

2

1 all rhyme
2 all start with '**s**' sound
3 contain short vowel '**a**': three-letter words
4 end with '**n**'
5 contain short vowel '**u**'
6 all have silent letters
7 start with '**sl**'
8 end with '**nd**': contain four letters
9 all rhyme
10 all start with '**l**' sound
11 all start with '**j**'/**dz**/sound
12 compound words
13 all contain '**r**'
14 all start and end with the same sounds e.g. **dead**
15 all end with '**s**' sound

3

1 all start with '**fr**' blend
2 all contain '**st**' blend
3 all have '**er**' second syllable
4 all contain '**or**'
5 four syllables
6 all have **in-** prefix
7 all start with '**f**' sound
8 all start with '**l**' blend
9 three syllables
10 all contain **ant**
11 all contain '**ar**' vowel
12 all start with '**h**' sound
13 all start with '**wh**' sound
14 five syllables
15 three letters are re-ordered to make a new word

Teacher Resources

Teacher Resource List

. . . .

Children's Books

What's in a sound or Talking about sounds
Crocodile Beat, Gail Jorgensen, Omnibus
Mrs. Armitage on Wheels, Quentin Blake, Picture Lions
Night Noises, Mem Fox, Ill. Terry Denton, Omnibus

Sound–Letter Link
Animal Parade — A Wildlife Alphabet, Jakki Wood, Hodder & Stoughton
City Seen From A to Z, Rachel Isadora, Mulberry Books
First Steps, John Burningham, Candlewick Press
John Birmingham's Alphabet Book, Walker Books
K is for Kiss Goodnight, Jill Sardegna, Picture Yearling
Mog's Amazing Birthday Caper, Judith Kerr, Collins
A Prairie Alphabet, Jo Bannatyne-Cugnet, Tundra Books
Richard Scarry's ABC World Book, Collins
Brian Wildsmith's ABC, Oxford University Press
You're Adorable, Martha Alexander, Candlewick Press

Rhyme
Anna Banana — 101 Jump-Rope Rhymes, Joanne Cole, Beech Tree Books
Crocodile Beat, Gail Jorgensen, Omnibus
Each Peach, Pear, Plum, Janet and Allan Ahlberg, Fontana Picture Lions
Dirty Beasts, Roald Dahl, Picture Puffin
Doctor Knickerbocker and Other Rhymes, David Booth, Kids Can Press
A Dragon in a Wagon, Lynley Dodd, Picture Puffin
The Eleventh Hour — A Curious Mystery, Graeme Base, Viking Kestrel
Gimme a Break, Rattlesnake!, Sonja Dunn, Pembroke Publishers
Hairy McClarey from Donaldson's Dairy, Lynley Dodd, Picture Puffin
The Jolly Christmas Postman, Allan Ahlberg, Heinemann
The Jolly Postman, Allan Ahlberg, Heinemann
Noisy Nora, Rosemary Wells, Fontana Picture Lions
Oranges and Lemons, Karen King, Oxford University Press
Pat-A-Cake and Play Rhymes, Joanna Cole & Stephanie Calmenson, Mulberry Books
Primary Rhymerry, Sonja Dunn, Pembroke Publishers
Revolting Rhymes, Roald Dahl, Picture Puffin
Round and Round the Garden, Sarah Williams, Oxford University Press
What Do You Do With a Kangaroo?, Mercer Mayer, Scholastic